A Better Place

A Better Place

Pati Navalta Poblete

NOTHING
BUT THE
TRUTH,
LLC

SAN FRANCISCO

Published in 2018 by Nothing But The Truth, LLC
NothingButTheTruth.com
Nothing But The Truth name and logo are trademarks of Nothing But The Truth Publishing, LLC.

LIBRARY OF CONGRESS CATALOGING-IN-PUBLICATION DATA
A Better Place
By Pati Navalta Poblete

Library of Congress Control Number: 2017919483

ISBN: 978-1-946706-99-7 (Paperback)
ISBN: 978-1-946706-00-3 (E-Book)

Printed in the United States of America
2018
Cover design by Grace Jang
First Edition

For Robby

Contents

Part Two

Looking Back

August 17, 2016.

As I write this, it is two months shy of the two-year anniversary of the death of my son, Robby, and one month shy of the scheduled preliminary hearing on his murder case. Four suspects have been in custody now for nearly a year, and it will be the first time that I will face them since they took my son's life. But this is not a story about the details of my son's death or what led to it. In truth, I have never read the police report, nor did I watch or read the news about his killing. I once caught a glimpse of a news article with a picture of his shiny Dodge Ram at the crime scene. I was with him as he signed the papers at the dealership less than a month before he was killed. I took a picture of him by that truck once the purchase was made, not knowing that would be the last picture taken of him. Not knowing that truck would one day be considered evidence.

The jury trial will begin sometime in 2017. The exact timing moves around, depending on numerous factors—defense attorneys, caseloads—dragging our raw emotions along with it. It will be there that I will hear the brutal details of his death. Amy Harris, the victim advocate assigned to our family by the DA's office, advises me there is video evidence, and that I should brace myself. She assures me that I don't have to attend. But who will represent my son? If all the jury sees are the crying mothers of the suspects, how will they know that Robby was taken from a family? These are thoughts that can easily consume me. So for now, I can only think of today, as I have every day since the day he was killed.

I write this now not because I have fully healed, but because I continue to do so. This is not a self-help or how-to book. There is no "how-to" when it comes to recovering from such a tragic loss. This is my story of how losing my son to gun violence shattered my world, my faith, my sense of community. And how I was able to rebuild my life through my son's sense of adventure, fearlessness, and love for life. As difficult as it is to write this story, I know that for those who have suffered their own tragedies it will be just as difficult to read. I've come to realize that the most deeply wounded among us are the most vulnerable to other people's suffering. We feel our own tears searing down our faces, our own hearts breaking, our own worlds crumbling when we see other people experiencing pain. Because we've been there. We are there. We know what it's like. But I also know that there is power in baring our broken hearts. As we share our stories, we realize that we are not alone, and that we are more connected than we can imagine. As parents, as children, as human beings, there is a common denominator of love. Even people we deem as incapable of loving love. And it's because of this that we feel pain. What we do with that pain has a ripple effect beyond our comprehension. Tragedies born of hatred, ignorance and greed happen every day. But there are also stories of kindness, empathy, forgiveness and healing. This story bears both. I could not have fully understood the latter without suffering the former—though I wish that weren't the case. Maya Angelou once said, "there is no greater burden than carrying an untold story." I wish to lay down my burden, and in doing so, help others lay down their own.

But first, the beginning.

Robby died in the same city where he was born: Vallejo, California, located in the northern region of the San Francisco Bay Area. Other than visiting the cemetery on the outskirts of the city where he was laid to rest, I have yet to return after calling it home for more than three decades. My therapist says this is part of my PTSD. I am not able to disassociate the city from his killing, and in some ways I hold it responsible. This, I'm told, is common. I also hold myself responsible: *We should have moved a long time ago.*

⤺

The smell of our newly built home was intoxicating. Carpet, paint, wood. Even the taupe grout between the burnt-orange tiles seemed to emanate an exotic scent. We had never lived in a new home before, and my mom was floating from room to room, placing boxes in their appropriate places. Finally, she and my dad found a city where they could lay down some roots. Since emigrating from the Philippines in 1967, nothing really felt like "home"— unfriendly neighbors, too far from work, unsafe neighborhood, no other Filipinos. But Vallejo was different. My dad said it would be a better place for us—him; my mom; my younger brother, Chris; and all four of our grandparents, who lived with us. Known mostly as a blue-collar city, it was affordable enough for them to purchase a home in a new development, yet economically promising enough for my dad to eventually open his own small business. It was 1980. I was 11 years old.

At the economic and social epicenter of Vallejo was the Mare Island Naval Shipyard, which at its peak in World War II was one of the busiest shipyards in the world. When our family moved to the city, the shipyard was still its lifeblood. Our new neighbors, the Robertsons, were brought to Vallejo from the Midwest because of Mare Island, and every morning I would watch Mr. Robertson walk to his car in a crisp, white uniform and officer cap. In the morning light, he was practically glowing. He and his wife had two young children—Allison and James—both with shiny golden hair, deep blue eyes and rosy cheeks. A few months after we moved in, the Robertsons asked me to babysit for them for a dollar an hour—mostly during the weekends or when Mrs. Robertson would go for her early morning run. I immersed myself in their American Dream. By the mid-1980s, the shipyard employed about 10,000 people and contributed approximately $500 million to the city's annual economy. My parents had opened their own real estate office, and as Vallejo continued to develop and attract new families, their business continued to expand as well.

Vallejo truly was a better place for our family. Over the next decade my parents made many friends and established themselves in the community. Real estate was booming and new developments were popping up in every vacant corner of the city. I went through elementary, middle and high school there, leaving only to attend college at the University of California in Davis. But I came right back after graduating in 1993.

That's when everything changed.

By then I had gotten married and had two small children—Robby, who was about to turn two, and Julie, a newborn. I took a job as a copy editor at the local newspaper, Vallejo Times-Herald, for $9.75 an hour. My husband, Ruben, and I were in the process of buying our first home, a foreclosed property that was selling for $142,451.

Built in 1977, our home was far from the new house my parents bought. We tore out the carpet, which was heavily stained. The paint was cracked and peeling. The major appliances all needed to be replaced. There was water damage under the kitchen sink. A hole remained in the master bathroom shower, whether from a bullet or a rock, we didn't know. But it was ours, and we were thrilled to be homeowners.

That same year, the U.S. Department of Defense released a lengthy list recommending the closure of 33 major U.S. military bases, which many attributed to the end of the Cold War. The list would have gone largely unnoticed in my personal and professional circles were it not for one thing: Mare Island was on it. This became the major story in our local newsroom. What would it mean for the city's economy? Where would all the families go? How would the city ever recover?

President Bill Clinton approved the recommendation, setting off a tectonic shift in the city—spiked homicide rate, robberies, auto thefts, unemployment, business closures, a downtown area heavily dotted with drugs and prostitution. At the newspaper, we ran headlines every day on the latest homicide: *Killing Marks No. XX for Vallejo.* It had become formulaic. Representatives of the Chamber of Commerce and the Realtors Association would call and complain, saying we were damaging the city's image and destroying business. They pleaded with us to stop running the homicide numbers in the headlines or they would pull their advertising dollars.

I would make my 10-minute commute home from working the swing shift every night, driving along the main strip where I'd see the same prostitutes rounding the corners, trolling the various taco trucks and searching for work. The newspaper was at the heart of the high-crime area in the southern part of the city, not far from Mare Island. Our home was on the northern end, filled with many families directly impacted by the base closure. My father-in-law was among them. He and my mother-in-law had lived the nomadic naval life for decades with their three children—Lourdes, Loreili and Ruben—moving from South Carolina to Florida to Illinois to Tennessee to Alaska to California's Mare Island. We bought a home within walking distance from theirs so my mother-in-law could help with Robby and Julie while Ruben and I worked.

Despite the city's growing uncertainties, these were hopeful years for our young family. Robby had more energy and strength than any child his age we had ever seen. We'd often have to find ways to temper this energy since he developed bronchial asthma when he was just three months old. Perhaps the only thing more active than his body was his mind. His questions never seemed to end, and over time his questions and statements became shockingly philosophical for a young child. At just two years old he showed an intense spirituality, always holding on to a small figure of Saint Jude, the patron saint of hope and impossible causes, which his grandmother gave him. Saint Jude, he said, would always protect him.

Once, he pointed to a statue of the Santo Niño (Spanish for the Christ Child) on his grandmother's altar and said, "I saw him, Mama! I saw him!" He could barely contain his excitement, stomping his foot to emphasize his words.

"Where?" she responded, playing along. "Where did you see the Santo Niño?"

"We were playing together in my room!" he answered.

From that moment on, my mother-in-law believed Robby was special, that he had a direct connection with the spiritual world. I came to believe that I was mothering an old soul, and I marveled at his mind and heart. *What will he become?*, I wondered, as all parents do.

But Rome was burning. The city's homicide rate tripled to a record 30 in 1994. At the time, Vallejo's population was 113,129. The only other city comparable in population size that exceeded the number of homicides was Inglewood, adjacent to South Central Los Angeles, with 49 slayings.

With congressional approval, Mare Island officially closed in the spring of 1996, ending 142 years of its existence in Vallejo.

The number of killings decreased from that record year, but the city continued to struggle in the wake of the closure for the next decade. While Vallejo was able to attract some new businesses, Mare Island sat largely vacant and dilapidated—a cruel reminder of what the city once was, and what it had become.

Then came the major municipal blows. In 2004, California Gov. Arnold Schwarzenegger signed a bill stripping the Vallejo Unified School District governing board's powers after a financial scandal led to the need for a $60 million state loan, one of the largest school bailouts in state history. I had been working as a writer and editor for the San Francisco Chronicle by then, going on five years. Robby was 13 and in middle school at the time. Julie was 11 and in her last year of elementary school. The drastic measure made me question whether we should move to an area with better schools—schools that weren't being run by the state. But low interest rates that year drove the Bay Area real estate market to record levels, making it difficult to compete financially with other buyers. And by this time, my marriage had come to an end.

In 2008, when both of the kids were in high school, Vallejo became the largest city in America to declare bankruptcy. The city of now 117,000 was hit especially hard by the weak housing market and rising public employee salaries and benefits. This meant cuts—deep cuts. Most notably in the Vallejo Police Department. The city eventually slashed 33 percent of its police force. When interviewed by Bloomberg, Robert Nichelini, then Vallejo's police chief, stated: "When you have half the number of people, you can only do half the amount of work." Once again, crime was on the rise in a city that had yet to find its equilibrium.

There were 24 homicides in Vallejo in 2013, marking the highest number of homicides the city had seen since that record year in 1994.

In 2014, there were 18 homicides.

My son was No. 14.

Part One

Part One

Shock

Chapter 1

The Call

The lawn at Cornerstone Sonoma was bookended by a Pinot Noir vineyard on one end and a reflecting pond with clusters of pastel water lilies on the other. Rows of white chairs had already been set out in preparation for a sunset wedding, with a winding path leading to a simple, vine-covered arch under which the couple would exchange their vows. Lining the lawn were tall olive trees, providing a natural light show as the sun filtered through their leaves, shimmying in the soft wind. After the ceremony, guests could follow a garden trail to a massive white tent where dinner would be served. A beautiful, rustic barn stood nearby, surrounded by funky art installations and architectural gardens. This is where the dancing would be.

"I love it," I told Cicero.

I had lost count of how many years we'd been engaged, or even together. We were friends and colleagues for years at the San Francisco Chronicle before our relationship evolved into something more. The transition happened so organically that we could never determine when it was that we officially became a couple. It didn't seem to matter to either of us, but people were starting to ask questions. *When are you going to set a date? Where is it going to be? How many people are you inviting?*

5

Robby and Julie had grown attached to him, having known him now for almost a decade. Cicero had never married or had any children of his own, though he loved kids and played a big role in raising his nephews and nieces. Because of this, he interacted with Robby and Julie with ease—never wanting to take Ruben's place in their lives, but instead was happy to lend an ear, offer advice and go on adventures with them. They called him "Keyya"—a term of respect and endearment carried over from his own nieces and nephews. "Are you and Keyya ever going to get married?" they'd ask. Robby was now 23, and Julie 21. Cicero and I purchased our first home together in the neighboring city of Fairfield in July 2013, after living together for more than five years. We decided that maybe it was time to finally get married.

September 21, 2014, could not have been a more perfect day. That Sunday was the last official day of summer, and Mother Nature put on her finest for the finale. Julie had already left to spend the day with her friends, and I texted Robby at 8:57 a.m. to join Cicero and me as we prepared to head out to the wine country.

"Do you want to come with me and Keyya to Sonoma later?" I messaged. "We're going to see this place where we might have our wedding. We will provide food if you come. We're leaving about 12:45."

"Thanks," he texted back at 11:12 a.m. "But I'm going in early [to work] tonight so I have to sleep. That's cool, I hope you guys like it."

Robby was working with Ruben at Genentech, a biotech company where he was brought on as a temporary employee. He started out learning how to rebuild valves for the manufacturing process. But he worked at such warp speed that he often found himself with hours of downtime. One day, he wandered into the facility's welding room and began learning how to weld. People were shocked to hear he had no prior training. It didn't take long before he was working on custom projects that were normally commissioned to outside contractors. He would go in early for every shift, hoping to learn more so he could get hired as a permanent, full-time employee alongside his dad. Before he knew it, he had racked up so many extra hours that he had enough for a down payment for his own truck.

He called me from the dealership asking if I could meet him. I walked over to look at his choice, an enormous Dodge Ram 1500—so massive it was called the "Big Horn Edition." It matched Robby's own stature. I took a picture of him standing by it after the purchase was over, still holding the freshly signed papers in his left hand, squinting his eyes in the sunlight and offering a shy smile.

This was a turning point in his life, professionally and personally. This was his first major purchase as a working man and I could see the immense look of pride on his face. Ruben and I remained good friends, and in fact lived within 10 minutes of each other to make it easier for the kids to go between houses. Robby and Ruben were now commuting together every day, and Robby was eager to show his dad what he could do. In turn, Ruben began seeing beyond his son's wake of dirty dishes and trail of laundry at home. And what emerged was a hardworking man who had a natural talent for welding, with an ease and confidence about him that he had never seen before. This meant a lot to Robby, who had become far more outgoing in recent years and wanted to share his new interests with the both of us.

With me, he shared his love of cooking, books, music and his desire to travel and learn about other cultures. We carved out a day so we could apply for his passport, in hopes of traveling to India in the near future. I had already been to India twice on business, but he wanted to see a side of the country that I had never seen. At the time, he was practicing yoga and meditation and wanted to visit ashrams in different parts of the country, where he could learn more about the practices in the Indian tradition.

With his dad, he shared his diverse hobbies and passions: cycling, archery, target shooting, boats, skateboarding, and surfing. Some interests had nothing to do with either of us, and he always looked forward to enlightening us with his newfound knowledge.

But there was something about a son wanting to show his father that he was becoming his own man and he was at that point. I understood this clearly one day when he dropped by after work.

"Dad told me he was proud of me," he said. He was exhausted and sprawled out on the couch, staring at the ceiling. There was tenderness in his voice, contentment in his expression. I knew that he would never forget those words from his father, and that working together would further strengthen their bond.

It was no surprise then that he chose to skip our wedding-planning day so he could go in to work early. He had been preparing for important interviews, which would bring him closer to getting hired full time. So Cicero and I left the house that day, determined to come back with a location and date—and we did.

After walking the grounds and agreeing this was where we wanted to get married, Cicero and I met with the event planner and secured April 18, 2015, for our wedding. Located on site was a cafe where we decided to have lunch before heading home. I was sitting at a shaded table while Cicero waited for our orders inside, when my heart began beating harder and faster. I placed my right hand over my chest, wondering if I was just excited over finalizing our plans. But that wasn't it. Something felt *wrong*.

◟

The sun still shone high when we made it home around 4:00 p.m. I decided to make boeuf bourguignon to mark the special day. The dish required at least three and a half hours, but securing a wedding site and date was something to celebrate, and Robby and Julie always loved when I made the dish. "Not just boeuf bourguignon," I'd tell them. "*Julia Child's* boeuf bourguignon," mimicking Amy Adams in the movie *Julie & Julia*. I brought out the ingredients one by one: beef, pearl onions, carrots, flour, tomato paste, garlic, red wine, and beef broth. I scanned the cluttered counter as I tied an apron around my waist. Cicero came in with the mail and I saw that the first bill for Robby's truck had come. For me, this marked the official beginning of his adulthood: his very own bill.

"Your first car payment bill has arrived," I texted him at 4:28 p.m. "Come here after work tomorrow to get some boeuf bourguignon and you can get your bill."

"Okay," he quickly responded.

I brought out the heavy Dutch oven and began chopping the strips of bacon and prepping the rest of the ingredients before starting the lengthy cooking process. An hour had passed before I glanced at my cellphone again, checking to see if Julie had sent me any messages. I saw that I had a missed call from Ruben's mom. She left a message on my voicemail.

Robby was shot!
Robby was shot!

⌐

I can only describe what happened next in bits and pieces. Flashes and blackouts. Life and death. And limbo. Imagine the earth beneath you opening up and swallowing you whole. Imagine feeling everything good inside you—love, joy, kindness, trust, security, hope—burning and scorching to embers, giving way to fear, desperation, anguish and helplessness. Imagine being trapped in your worst nightmare, knowing that you will never wake from it. Imagine feeling truly abandoned—by God, by the universe, by humanity. Imagine all of that—and imagine it being far worse.

I know I screamed. I know that Cicero came running out of Julie's bedroom where he was painting her wall. I know I fumbled with my phone trying to call anyone and everyone, but nobody was answering. I must have reached someone, though I don't remember whom, because for some reason we were now in the car heading toward the freeway.

Fairfield and Vallejo were connected by a mere 20-minute stretch of highway on Interstate 80. But on this day, there was traffic. I cried frantically as Cicero tried desperately to weave in and out of the congestion. I remember thinking that we would get a call at any moment letting us know what hospital Robby had been transported to. "Why aren't they calling?" I screamed. "Where are they bringing him?"

Instead, I got a call from Julie.

"Mom," she wailed. "Mom. Mom."

And I knew.

When you go into shock, when your heart is shattered and pulverized, when a part of you is taken so suddenly and brutally, something takes over. I let out a primal moan unlike any sound I had ever heard coming from my body. In my mind, I was saying "No!" But it didn't sound like that. It was a guttural, wounded roar of a lioness losing her cub. For months, that sound haunted me. "But why would you fear that?" my therapist would later ask me. "That sound is what unites us all. It came from our instinct to protect, to love, to mourn. It's what makes us human."

My body had crumpled over in the car. I pounded on the dashboard until my hands were red and raw. All my pain, anguish, confusion and helplessness were trapped in the claustrophobic confines of our car for 30 minutes.

When we finally pulled up to the location, I raced out, frantically looking for what, I didn't know. All I could see were yellow police tape, police cars with flashing lights, officers, crowds gathering to see what was going on. I fell to my knees.

For the next six hours we sat, Ruben, Julie, Cicero, my in-laws, as the police asked us questions. A chaplain with the Vallejo Police Department found his way to me, speaking tenderly and slowly.

"Would you like me to offer a prayer for your son?"

I nodded my head, not knowing, not understanding. Not believing that any of this was real.

We sat. We sat. We sat. Until the sun faded away and darkness encircled us.

But he has to go to work, I kept thinking. *He has to go in early for work.*

Chapter 2

Nine Days

Following Catholic tradition, the novena (prayer) for the dead began less than 24 hours after Robby's death, setting off nine consecutive days of communal prayer. There were more than 100 people packed into our house the first night, sitting, standing, leaning. People I hadn't seen since high school. Relatives. Neighbors. People I used to work with. My closest friends. People who I never knew cared. I sat frozen at the end of our couch, clutching Robby's worn T-shirt that I found on his bed, taking in his scent with every inhalation. They came to me, one by one.

I'm so sorry.

He's with God.

What happened?

Why was he there?

Who did this?

We'll find them.

God wanted Robby with him.

He's in a better place. He's in a better place.

I didn't want to hear it. I was inconsolable, collapsing into the arms of whoever extended them. I couldn't bear the expressions on their faces, filled with pity, awkwardness and questions. I had no answers, and it didn't matter. I didn't read the articles or watch the news. I didn't want to see my son's face under the same headline I had written so many times in the newsroom. Not my son. I didn't know who shot him, or why. I didn't care. The answers would not bring Robby back.

I can't recall the minute details of those first nine days. I was in a state of shock. Things were happening around me, but my head was still stuck at the crime scene. When the detectives finally told us we should go home, it was near midnight. I went straight to Robby's room and fell onto his bed, wanting to capture whatever was left of him. I screamed his name, hoping my cries would reach wherever he had gone. Where had he gone? What happens when someone dies such a tragic death? Is their soul left wandering and in shock? My maternal instinct was to find him, save him, and bring him home. But it was too late.

"All you can do is pray," my mom said.

But I *had* prayed. I prayed from the day my kids were born. I wasn't a devout Catholic, but I believed in God and I believed in kindness and forgiveness. I prayed for my children's happiness, their success, their health. I prayed for their safety. But God didn't hear those prayers. In my state of shock, I wasn't angry at whoever killed my son. I was angry at God for allowing it to happen.

"We have to pray for his soul," my mom said. I didn't have the strength to respond. How could I pray when I no longer had faith?

Ruben's sister, Loreili, led the guests in reciting the rosary with the intention of guiding and elevating Robby's soul to heaven and out of purgatory. I watched her fingers roll across each bead of the Hail Mary as the group chanted the same response after each line: *Have mercy on the soul of Robby.* I was grateful for the people there, but each line of prayer added to my trauma.

My Jesus, through your bloody sweat in the garden.

My Jesus, through the blow You received on Your Sacred face.

My Jesus, through the cruel scourging you endured.

My Jesus, through the crown of thorns that pierced Your head.

My Jesus, through Your carrying on the Cross on the path of bitterness.

My Jesus, through Your face with blood which you allowed to be imprinted on the veil of Veronica.

My Jesus, through Your Holy Body nailed on the Cross.

My Jesus, through Your Hands and Feet pierced with cruel nails.

My Jesus, through Your Sacred side pierced with the lance from which flowed blood and water.

Prayers were supposed to help comfort and strengthen. These words provoked violent, jarring images that forced me to imagine my son's own brutal death. Blood, suffering, pain. I closed my eyes, letting out a faint, steady note to drown out the noise.

Forgive those who trespass against us...

I didn't even know whom I was forgiving.

After the prayer, I looked up to see my mom ladling food from a large pot into small paper bowls while my aunt handed them out to people. "What did she make?" I asked my cousin. She seemed surprised by my question. Why would I even care what was being served? "Uh, I think she said it's beef stew or something," she responded, blowing her nose. I realized my mom had found all the ingredients I left on the counter before I got the call. I pictured her tossing everything in the pot and leaving it to fend for itself, rather than going through the methodical layering of each flavor. And all I could think was: *That wasn't supposed to be beef stew. That was supposed to be boeuf bourguignon. Julia Child's boeuf bourguignon. None of these people are supposed to be here. I was planning my wedding and Robby was supposed to be here paying his car bill, packing his lunch for work the next day. None of this is happening.*

The crowd grew steadily in size as news got out. Some nights, the house was so crowded that guests were forced to stand in the garage or backyard during prayer. I stared at the altar that now faced the family room. More than a dozen framed pictures of Robby: graduations, family trips, birthdays. The day we brought him home from the hospital. Flickering candles illuminated his smiling face, only to darken, then light up again. Here one moment, gone the next. Flowers, a statue of the Virgin Mary. A crucifix. *What is happening?* I kept wondering.

You have to eat. You have to stay strong. Family members continued making plates of food for me, but I couldn't stomach anything. I cried so much during the day that I was retching and dry heaving. By the time people came for prayer, I was dazed and exhausted.

Julie was exhausted too, but she kept busy, scanning pictures, going to the printers, making arrangements for the wake. She was constantly surrounded by her friends, who had formed a committee of sorts, ensuring that she was never alone. She couldn't stand the prayers. She would have panic attacks and retreat to her room. I didn't blame her. I didn't want to be there either. She created an online memorial and donation page for her brother. Within minutes the messages and donations came pouring in, locally and abroad. I never could have imagined the number of people who came to support us, donated money, sent cards and flowers, brought food. People who came to just sit and hold my hand. Never in my life had I experienced such an outpouring of love and kindness.

The community carried our family, and in the midst of our tragedy, I felt gratitude. I knew I could build on that to find my way back, someday, but I needed help. And I no longer believed that God or the church was the answer.

Don't worry. An eye for an eye. A tooth for a tooth, a close relative whispered in my ear, assuming this would comfort me. I felt my skin crawl. I didn't care if he was quoting the Bible; revenge was not what I wanted. I wanted my son.

Other people assumed I was watching the news and discussed details of the case. Their race. Number of suspects. *Suspects?* There was more than one? I ran upstairs and screamed into my pillow. I didn't want to know.

Each night I sat at the far end of our couch. We pushed the dining table against the wall, arranging Robby's pictures and flowers on top of it, and making space for four rows of chairs to accommodate guests. On one of the nights, I felt a warm hand press into mine. I looked up to see an unfamiliar woman, hunched over by age. She placed a small leaflet in my hand and said, "Read this when you can. It will help you." I thanked her and placed the leaflet on my nightstand when everyone had gone. It wasn't until a few days later that I picked it up and began to read. On the cover was a picture of Jesus kneeling. I turned the page and read the first line:

Suffering is God's Will.

I ripped the leaflet to shreds.

There is a need for some people to say something—*anything*. Pain and grief, especially under such tragic circumstances, are too uncomfortable. So their instinct is to fill the awkward void. To make you stop crying. To provide answers and make sense of the inexplicable. To make things *normal*. I was told repeatedly that this was "God's will" or "God's plan." I was told that I shouldn't question what happened because this is what God wanted. *God doesn't give you more than you can handle.*

Bullshit. What kind of God was this? Why would it be his will to have my son gunned down? Was our suffering supposed to make us more worthy? A woman whom I had never met before told me, "I almost lost my son, too. But we were blessed." What did that make us? What did that make Robby? I never realized before how offensive, judgmental and elitist that word was: *Blessed.* As if good things only happen to God's chosen ones. The rest of us are just screwed.

"God does not love me," I told my mom. "There is no God."

But I was in a spiritual Catch-22. If God did not exist, then how could I pray for Robby's soul? If God did not exist, and there was no heaven, then where did Robby go? And if none of it existed, did that mean I would never see my son again?

I had to have faith that my son was in the hands of a kind and loving God, even if the circumstances of his death told me otherwise. If there was a God, I was angry at him. And yet I needed him to keep Robby alive, in some form. I needed to believe he was still out there.

I needed to believe he was in a better place.

Chapter 3

Saying Goodbye

I ran my index finger down each electric pleat on my black chiffon skirt, trying to steady my trembling hands. I was running out of black clothes, and this dress still had the price tags attached to it.

I bought the dress in Tokyo just a month earlier during a business trip for Global Footprint Network, where I had been working since October 2008. The Oakland-based international research organization helped national governments understand how to monitor and manage their natural resources using a unique resource accounting tool called the Ecological Footprint. This methodology was created by the organization's co-founder, Mathis Wackernagel, who was now my boss. This was unlike any job I had ever had. Prior to this I was working at the American Cancer Society across from the state Capitol in Sacramento, but the hour-plus commute from Vallejo was costing me nearly $500 a month. I needed something closer that still allowed me to use my skills in writing and advocacy. Global Footprint Network was approximately 35 minutes from my house, and on days when traffic was particularly bad I had the option of taking BART, our metro system in the Bay Area. The job allowed me to travel to countries I never imagined I'd set foot in—Russia, Cambodia, Bangladesh,

Peru, India, Indonesia, Switzerland, Australia, China, Thailand, France and so many more. Though I was first hired as a communications director, within two years I was promoted to the Asia regional director, giving presentations to representatives at the highest levels of government and consulting with them on their sustainability policies. I traveled about 35 percent of the year, a majority of the time alone. But because we were gaining more projects in Asia I was given a full-time researcher, Katsunori "Katsu" Iha, based in Japan, and a project development coordinator, Phillip Fullon, based in Manila.

This time I was sent to Japan to meet with several agencies and Katsu flew in from his hometown in Okinawa to join me. He and I rode the famous Shinkansen high-speed bullet train from Tokyo to Kyoto to give a presentation at a research institute. Afterward, a local professor took us to see the Shimogamo Shrine, one of the oldest Shinto shrines in Japan and a designated historic monument in Kyoto. Following the Shinto custom, we washed our hands and mouths at a trough placed in front of the temple gates, using a bamboo ladle to transfer the cool water onto our cupped hands.

"Bow two times, clap two times, then bow again," Professor Wada instructed, pointing to a small shrine tucked between lush trees and shrubs. "Mothers pray for their children here."

I walked toward the shrine, trying to remember the instructions. *Bow twice. Clap twice. Bow again.* I lowered my head before the shrine, inhaling the heavy scent of sandalwood wafting from the burning incense, and offered a prayer for Robby and Julie. My mind wandered thinking of how I hoped to bring them back someday so they could witness these different rituals. I prayed that my kids would be able to see the world as they got older. I raised my head and rejoined my colleagues.

"Very good. Now your kids have blessing from Kyoto," said the professor.

We took the train back to Tokyo that day, exhausted from the heat wave that smothered Japan that week. Tokyo station was a maze of eateries and boutique shops. I walked along the winding paths, bobbing and weaving through the throngs of locals coming home from work. Drinks, rice crackers, and bento boxes lined the storefronts. I turned the corner toward my next train when I saw the black chiffon dress hanging in a boutique window. It looked light and sweet with its electric pleats, a throwback to Audrey Hepburn circa the '60s. I gauged the time to make sure I wouldn't miss my train and darted into the store. It was a snug fit, but I was committed to going on a diet when I returned home. International travel required a lot of meetings over meals and it wreaked havoc on my waistline.

Maybe I'll wear this out to a nice dinner, I thought.

Now it hung loosely on my dwindling frame, and I was wearing the dress to the mortuary.

Six days had passed since September 21, and we still had not seen Robby. His body was considered evidence and was brought to the coroner's for an autopsy. Ruben and I spent those days making the funeral arrangements with Loreili's support. While she was also grieving, she graciously stepped in and offered to help us with the impossible task of burying our son. She came with us to every meeting, notebook in hand, as Ruben and I sat shell-shocked, too distraught to make decisions or retain any information. The mortuary, the casket, the cemetery, his gravestone.

At each stop we were asked the same question, "Is your son the one who was in the news? The one who was shot?" Ruben and I would lower our heads and nod.

"I hope they catch the people who did this to him," said one woman sternly as we finished choosing the readings for Robby's funeral Mass. Up until then, she had been sitting patiently, gently guiding us through our options of readings and songs for the service. She and the woman next to her were Lazarus ministers for the church, tasked with helping family members with the liturgy of the funeral Mass and offering them support in their time of grief.

"How did your son die?" she asked as we gathered our papers to leave. Ruben and I looked at each other, not knowing how to answer. "Was he the young man in the news?" she asked. We both began crying. "I hope they catch the people who did this to him."

It was all so surreal—planning his funeral with everyone knowing about his death from the local news. We went through the motions in a haze of denial fueled by disbelief. "We shouldn't be doing this," said Ruben as we flipped through a catalog of tombstones. "He was supposed to do this for us when he got older. We're not supposed to be doing this for him."

Now it was time to finally see our son, and I was afraid. I didn't know if he would look the same. I was terrified that I would see fear or pain on his face—whatever emotion he felt when he was killed. But I had to see him. I had to see him to know that it was real.

A group of about 10 of us agreed to meet in the mortuary parking lot that morning so we could walk in together. I continued to fidget with my dress on the drive over, transporting my mind back to Tokyo and wishing I could just go back in time. How was I to know, as I stood before that tranquil shrine, the horror that awaited us just one month later? How was I to know when I bought that dress that I would be wearing it to see my son here, today, in this way?

My heart was throwing rapid punches against my chest, as if it were trying to escape my body before we got to the mortuary. It had been through enough. My mind traveled manically between space and time, realizing the situation, then escaping back to Tokyo. Hiding, realizing, hiding again.

When we finally pulled into the lot, I saw Ruben taking a long drag from his cigarette. He was up to smoking four packs a day.

Others were standing beside their cars, shrouded in black clothes, dark sunglasses and weary faces. The crunching sound of loose gravel beneath the tires sent a surge of panic through me. It was time.

⸙

Robby was laid to rest in a dark suit he had set out on his bed in preparation for his job interview. He spent months growing his hair out, perfecting his "man bun." I regretted telling him to get a haircut. I should have told him how handsome he looked. I should have complimented him everytime he marveled at his ability to pull back that bun. Thoughts like these cross your mind as you prepare to say goodbye.

I should have . . .
Why didn't I . . .
If only . . .
I'm so sorry.

I don't remember the details of that first day going into the mortuary. There are many details I don't remember and many that I wish I could forget. But I know that Robby had a look of peace on his face. He had the same look on his face as he did many mornings when I would wake him up for breakfast.

He's just sleeping, I thought to myself.

The prayers moved from our home to the mortuary, where the remaining two nights ended with people coming to the podium to share their stories of Robby. I learned more about him during those two nights than I ever had before.

I didn't know that he would regularly visit his friend's grandparents so he could help them at their care home. He would drop by and ask if they needed him to do any heavy lifting or any other chores that required a man of his size and strength.

I didn't know that he approached his sister's first boyfriend back in high school to give an "older-brother" warning to treat her right.

I learned about his long-distance bike ride from Vallejo to Oakland, then to Sacramento.

I learned the details of how he knocked on the door at the Vallejo Yacht Club to see if they'd allow him to be an honorary member. He took an interest in boats and wanted to learn more about them from the club members. He went on sailing trips with them, participated in their club events and planned on buying his own boat one day. Maybe he'd become an actual member and pay dues.

His Aunt Lourdes spoke of how he would go to her house after surfing all day at Ocean Beach in San Francisco. He'd go straight to their bathroom to shower, leaving piles of sand and the smell of ocean water in his wake.

My brother and one of his friends spoke of Robby's love of cooking. He spent hours smoking meat for a family barbecue contest, bemoaning the fact that he came in second place.

Everyone seemed to talk about how Robby would go to their homes and head straight to the kitchen to see what there was to eat. He loved to eat.

His boss talked about how hardworking he was. How he loved welding and worked faster and harder than most people he knew. He described Ruben looking in on Robby in the welding room and seeing his chest puff up with pride. "We were going to hire him as a full-time employee," he said. "There was no doubt. We were going to hire him." He lowered his head.

What a waste. What a horrible, horrible waste.

Some people couldn't get through their speeches through the tears. But there was laughter, too. On the last night at the mortuary, the night before the funeral, Julie pulled my arm and led me to the entrance. "I want to show you something," she said. When she finally stopped, I looked in front of me and saw a mix of my high school friends and college roommates—Margie and Valerie, who both moved back to Southern California after we graduated; Leila, Annamarie, Connie and Mellie, who remained local; and Cora, who now lived in Maui and traveled the farthest to be there. They were all my children's godmothers—all bridesmaids in my wedding when I married Ruben. And now they were all there as I prepared for the unimaginable, burying my son. They formed a circle around me in a group hug, each one of them sobbing.

The funeral service was a haze. Every pew in the church was filled with friends and loved ones, but all I saw was a sea of blurry faces. I sat between Julie and Cicero, directly in front of Robby's casket. At one point I felt Julie shifting in her seat, turning her head and lifting her arm. I didn't know what she was doing.

When the service was over, our family followed the casket out of the church as everyone looked at us. I turned to put my head on Cicero's shoulder as we walked and was hit with a powerful, flowery scent. It smelled like citrus and jasmine mixed with some kind of musk. I thought perhaps Cicero was wearing a new cologne.

We watched as the pallbearers carried the casket into the hearse before separating into our cars to head for the cemetery. "Did you smell barbecue in the church?" my brother asked. The question was so random that I stared back at him blankly. "We both smelled barbecue right when the service was over," he said, my sister-in-law, Sandy, nodding in agreement.

"No, I smelled your cologne," I told Cicero.

"I'm not wearing cologne," he replied.

Ruben's family then exited the church, embracing each of us. "Did you smell the ocean?" Lourdes asked. "There was a strong smell of the ocean after the service." We all looked at each other, confused.

"I smelled body odor," said Julie. "I was lifting my arm to see if it was me, but it wasn't. And it wasn't you, Mom. It was really strong."

During the eulogies, my brother focused on Robby's love of cooking, especially smoking and barbecuing meats. Lourdes spoke of how he loved to surf and how he would bring traces of the ocean back to their home afterward. Julie always joked with Robby that he needed a shower. Barbecue. Ocean. Body odor. Each person smelled something that they associated Robby with—and it was amazing.

"He's saying he's here," I said.

When it came time to lay him to rest, more than 200 people stood in the cemetery to say goodbye. His pallbearers removed the ti-leaf garlands they wore around their necks in honor of Robby's love for the Hawaiian culture and placed them one by one on his casket. I watched the people line up, each holding a flower as they walked past Robby to say their final goodbyes. A woman I worked with looked up from Robby's casket and looked over to me. She placed her right hand over her heart and blew a kiss toward me with her left hand. These are scenes I will never forget. In the face of hate, there is incredible love.

But the road ahead was long, and I didn't know how or if that feeling could sustain us. I knew that none of us would ever be the same again. Life would never be the same.

Where do we go from here?, I wondered.

We released 23 butterflies, one for each year of his life, watching them cluster and dissipate toward the bright blue sky. I closed my eyes, wishing I could fly with them.

We went home after that long day, drained of physical and emotional strength. A group of us headed up the stairs and into Robby's room. Julie picked up a small vial that was sitting on top of his dresser. "What's that?" I asked.

"This Egyptian oil or musk that he bought somewhere. He was using it as a cologne," she said. I walked over to smell it. The exact smell that overwhelmed me in the church.

It wasn't Cicero's scent I was smelling. It was Robby's.

Chapter 4

Send Me a Sign

My nightstand was covered with stacks of books—all focused on near-death experiences and stories of the afterlife. People who had suffered tragic accidents or were in comas due to severe medical conditions—some deeply religious, others atheists—all describing their brush with death and their experience on the other side. I needed to know if there was something else out there—where my son was and what he was experiencing. These stories pulled the curtain back on the unknown, enabling me to envision where Robby had gone.

There were recurring themes in each story, despite how different the authors' backgrounds were. One woman was a surgeon and suffered a major accident while whitewater rafting. She described her spirit leaving her body and actually seeing it there on the water as she seemed to move farther and farther away from it. She could hear the cries of her friends as they stayed with her body, begging her to wake up, but she was already on her way to something else. Someplace beautiful and peaceful that she didn't want to leave. Another man was in a car accident and fell into a coma. He described being in a dark space, not knowing where he was or how he got there. While he said it wasn't scary, it certainly wasn't pleasant. But he knew he had a choice—to stay in the darkness or will himself toward the light, which he did. It was there that he described a place of tranquility and beauty.

I was obsessed with these books, taking in as much as I could about the afterlife. All the authors described disappointment in having to return to their bodies on Earth, but had a profound realization that this life isn't all there is—and it certainly wasn't the grand finale. The authors all described a place so overwhelmingly beautiful and loving that there simply were no words that could adequately capture it. They recounted being everywhere at once and not having a sense of time. Feeling no pain or sorrow or regret, only love. Being reunited with lost loved ones and knowing that even though the families they left behind may be grieving, everything would be okay. This gave me some sense of relief. The thought of Robby roaming around confused, looking for us and missing us, kept tearing me up inside.

"What if he's looking for us?" I kept asking everyone. My body was stuck here, but I was desperately trying to reach the other side in hopes of finding my son. The only way I could do that was by reading about people who had been there.

In two weeks I had read eight different books on near-death experiences. *Don't ignore the signs*, read one of them. The wall between the living and the spiritual world was very thin, according to the book, and those in the spiritual world sometimes send signs to show they're okay.

A week after Robby's funeral, I started getting messages from his friends. Mark Marcelo, one of his closest friends, described having a very vivid dream about Robby. They were sitting in his truck in front of a house where a family party was being held. Mark looked at Robby and said, "Wait a minute, you're dead."

He said Robby started to laugh.

"No," Mark said, "I gave a eulogy at the mortuary. I know you're dead."

But Robby only smiled. "I'm still here," he said. "I'm right here."

Other people called and messaged me describing the same dream—Robby smiling, assuring them that he was still around. But I never got that dream, nor did Julie, Ruben or Cicero. We waited, but it never came.

So I began researching psychic mediums. I knew it sounded crazy, but I desperately wanted to connect with my son. I looked at different websites, searching for reviews and credentials. I didn't know what type of credentials I was looking for—anything to make them seem more legitimate. I spoke with three different mediums, each one describing something that would resonate with me—but a part of me felt like it was just my desperation forcing me to connect the dots.

I sense something in my . . . arm? My . . . chest? My . . . head? My . . . leg?

I'd wait until the body parts correlated with Robby's injuries and say, "Yes, that's him!"

And then they would continue:

He says he's sorry and to stop crying.

He says thank you for the flowers you brought him.

He says you heard a song that reminded you of him on the radio.

I'd start crying and answer, "Yes! He can see me! I did hear the song. I did bring him flowers!"

And then reasoning would kick in.

Of course I'm crying. Of course I'm bringing him flowers. Of course every song on the radio is going to remind me of him. *Sucker.*

I promised myself I was done, until I read a book by an author named Mark Anthony, a practicing attorney whose psychic medium powers were nationally recognized and respected. I did more research online after reading his book and found numerous videos of him giving readings.

Maybe he's the real deal, I thought.

He lived on the East Coast but was able to give readings by phone. It was at least a four-month wait to schedule a reading, but I put my name on the list. A month later, I received an email saying that Mr. Anthony would be available to do a reading for me. I asked Julie to join me since she, too, had been longing for signs from her brother. We started the call without saying anything other than our names. He explained the process to us:

Don't be quick to dismiss something if you don't understand it. It may come to you later, so take lots of notes. Sometimes those in the spirit world will find a way to confirm you've interpreted the message correctly by following up with a statement that is undeniably true. This is their way of saying, "Yes! You got it." Don't give any information about whom you're trying to contact; let the messages come through on their own.

We sat in Robby's room staring at phone, which was on speaker, each of us with a notebook and pen in hand, waiting for him to say something that meant anything to us.

He addressed Julie first, describing things that only she and her brother knew. "Shamrocks, he's saying shamrocks. Does that mean anything to you?" Julie began to smile and tear up at the same time.

"Yes," she said. "Ever since we were little I'd always look for four-leaf clovers, but I could never find them. Then when I visited him at the cemetery there were four-leaf clovers all around me by his grave. Nobody else could find them but me."

He went through a series of other extremely specific details of Robby's past, describing his ex-girlfriend and even specific names. "Is he okay?" we asked.

"Yes!" he answered. "He says that when he was on Earth he kind of kept to himself and did his own thing. But now he can be every-where and anywhere he wants. He's free." We were both crying in his room now.

"One more thing," he said, as our 60 minutes was coming to an end. "He wants you to write a book. He says to write a book about what it's like as a mother living through this kind of tragedy. *Write, write, write.* That's what he's saying."

⤳

I took off my reading glasses and rubbed my eyes. I had been reading now for three hours and it was just past 2:00 a.m. The book I had been reading described different ways our loved ones try to communicate with us from the other side—songs on the radio, birds or butterflies that seem to appear out of nowhere, pennies that seem to show up everywhere.

The story reminded me of the scene in *Ghost* when Patrick Swayze's spirit moved the penny up the door to show Demi Moore's character that he was really there. According to the book, there is something in pennies that makes it easier for spirits to manipu-late and move them. Spirits, after all, are made up of energy—and though they no longer had the physical strength that came with a body, they did possess a force through their energy. The phrase "pennies from heaven" suddenly made sense to me.

I placed my book and my glasses on top of my nightstand and turned off the light next to my bed, leaving the dim light in our bathroom on. I then heard a thud on the ground. I leaned over my bed and saw the outline of my glasses on the floor. *Strange*, I thought, picking them up and placing them back at the center of my nightstand. It was then that I heard another thud and realized that my dog had jumped off the bed. He only did that when he needed water in the middle of the night, so I waited to hear the tapping of his nails against the tiles of our bathroom where his water bowl was, but the sound never came. I called his name, and still nothing. I let out a sigh and leaned over to turn the light on, dragging myself out of bed. I looked around the room and found him on the floor on his belly, his two front legs stretched out in front of him. And sitting there between his two paws, as if he was presenting it to me, was one shiny penny.

Chapter 5

The Dark Night of the Soul

It was clear that I was suffering from more than grief.

I was sleep-deprived, and panic attacks prevented me from leaving the house or being alone. I had post-traumatic stress disorder (PTSD) mixed with depression and anxiety, and I didn't know how to separate one from the other. I didn't know what "normal" was for someone in this situation, or if normal even existed anymore. There were things that caused my heart to race, setting off a domino effect on my mental and physical states. Sweaty palms, the feeling of panic moving to my head, down my neck and spreading through my back like wildfire. Spinning head, followed by dizziness, a tightening in the chest and then panic. Pure panic. Was this depression, or was this something else? I started keeping a list.

Things I can't do:

- Watch TV or go to the movies (too many gun scenes and too much violence)
- Hear police sirens or look at police cars gathered in one place (flashbacks)
- Go anywhere with a lot of people and/or loud noises (general fear and anxiety)
- Look people in the eye (??)

- Drive (anxiety)
- Listen to anything about God (anger)
- Take walks alone (fear)
- Sleep with the lights off (same)
- Sleep for more than three hours (nightmares)
- Go to Vallejo, other than the cemetery (fear, anxiety, panic attacks, anger)
- Drive along the freeway we took on the way to the crime scene (same)
- Rest my head on Cicero's chest (sound of his heartbeat is traumatizing)
- Be alone (fear, anxiety, panic attacks)
- Talk about the wedding or getting married
- Listen to any music with lyrics (too painful)
- Stop bouts of crying
- See pictures of my friends with their children on social media

I knew I needed help, so I began researching nearby therapists under my insurance plan. This is how I came to find Marsha Maslan, a certified therapist whose list of specialties included: Anxiety/Panic Attacks, Depression, Family Issues, Grief/Loss/ Mourning, Post-Traumatic Stress Disorder, Social Anxiety Disorder and Traumatic Incident, among others.

Who brings you joy?
Julie
Who gives you peace?
Cicero
Who comforts you?
Oprah Winfrey
Oprah Winfrey? Wait, what was I saying? I wanted to retract my answer, but the therapist kept going.

Who gives you strength?

I decided to just run with it. "Maya Angelou."

Now I want you to close your eyes and bring them into the room, one by one. Imagine them surrounding you and giving you joy, peace, comfort, strength. How does that make you feel?

To my surprise, it actually worked. I imagined Oprah standing there with Maya next to her, locking arms with Cicero and Julie. Oprah and Maya were looking at me, nodding and smiling with that look they have. That look that says, "I've seen suffering, too, and I survived."

Next time you're somewhere and you have another panic attack, find somewhere to go, close your eyes, and imagine them surrounding you again. You can bring them into any room at any time.

Oprah and Maya helped me out of countless situations, leading Cicero and Julie in forming a protective bubble around me like fairy godmothers. They were there at the produce section of the grocery store, during car rides, when the phone would ring, when I was around strangers, at the cemetery.

Before coming to Marsha, I met with Richard, another therapist who specialized in grief. I used up his whole box of tissues that first day, telling him my story and Robby's story, recounting everything. At the end of the session, I blew my nose, wiped my eyes and looked up to see him sobbing in his chair. He explained that he lost his son years ago, and that's what led him to this practice. He wanted to help other grieving parents through their pain.

"There is a long road ahead," he said through his tears. "Literature refers to it as 'the dark night of the soul.'"

"When did your son die?" I asked.

"Almost 10 years ago."

My shoulders dropped and I fell back into his worn leather

couch, watching him sob into his own Kleenex. Ten years and he was still in as much pain as I was.

I looked at him and imagined the rest of my life.

This is it, I thought. *Things will never get better. He is me in 10 years, exactly where I am now.* A grieving parent, forever doomed to suffer the dark night of the soul.

I never saw Richard again, but I kept the term with me, to the point of near-obsession. When asked how I was doing, I'd sometimes tell people, "I am in the dark night of the soul," then walk away as if I had just told them I was going gluten-free.

In Catholicism, the "dark night of the soul" refers to a period of spiritual emptiness or abandonment that a person may experience in their journey toward a closer relationship with God. The soul is plunged in darkness, stripped of attachments, suffering, comfort, pleasure and sin. It is in this utter darkness that, ironically, the person is able to see the light: that we are nothing without God. Only then can we understand and appreciate the crosses that we bear in life and embrace them. The term originated from the poem "*La noche oscura del alma*," written by 16th-century Spanish poet and Roman Catholic mystic Saint John of the Cross. Again, suffering as a rite of passage.

Though centuries-old and steeped in religion, the term has also been used throughout secular literature, mostly in reference to periods of despair, confusion and hopelessness. Author Eckhart Tolle's interpretation of the phenomenon could have been a page from my diary:

The "dark night of the soul" is a term used to describe what one could call a collapse of a perceived meaning in life . . . an eruption into your life of a deep sense of meaninglessness. The inner state in some cases is very close to what is conventionally called depression. Nothing makes sense anymore, there's no purpose to anything. Sometimes it's triggered by some external event, some disaster perhaps, on an external level. The death of someone close to you could trigger it, especially premature death, for example if your child dies. Or you had built up your life, and given it meaning . . . and the meaning that you had given your life for some reason collapses.

In his explanation, Tolle describes a type of rebirth, where the person can emerge out of the darkness into a transformed state. Life has meaning again, but not the same meaning it once had. We are awakened to something more meaningful with a "deeper sense of purpose or connectedness." This was the most I could hope for.

I was determined not to become part of Richard's own therapy session, so after that first session with him I went home and looked through a long list of potential therapists. Marsha's online description of her focus areas read like a grocery list of my mental afflictions. Marsha had alternative treatments for PTSD, beyond mentally conjuring my protectors. But some treatments were at times too brutal to bear.

What do you see when you imagine what happened?

I had described the scene several times now, but from different vantage points. As a witness at the scene. As someone there to prevent the incident. As a stranger on a bus passing by. I still didn't know exactly what happened, but I knew enough for images—real and imagined—to seep into my nightmares like cancerous cells.

What do you see when you close your eyes at night?

I sat in front of her, eyes closed, both feet on the ground facing squarely toward her. She wouldn't let me cross my feet or my legs. She set a small device the size and shape of a Walkman on her desk with a headset and two wires attached to it. At the end of the wires were "pulsers" shaped like plastic packing peanuts.

I put the headset on and held a pulser in each hand as the device set off alternating audio tones and electric pulses in my palms. She changed the volume and the strength of the vibration, depending on how I reacted to different questions. This approach was called eye movement desensitization and reprocessing (EMDR) treatment, developed by American psychologist Francine Shapiro, Ph.D. In the late 1980s, it was considered a revolutionary method of helping patients overcome psychological trauma. The goal of this treatment was to have me describe and reprocess the information from my traumatic experience until it was no longer traumatic, or "psychologically disruptive."

As I recalled the traumatic events, Marsha would use the device to stimulate parts of my brain that may have gone into hiding during my shock. But the sudden vibrations made me anxious, and the alternating beeps in my ears made me want to scream. My nerves were so raw that I was perpetually on the verge of a mental breakdown.

So we tried another method, "emotional freedom techniques" (EFT), using tapping. Marsha tapped my knees—left, right, left, right—as I described recent situations that led to panic attacks.

I went to the grocery store and I had to walk slowly, peeking behind corners before going into an aisle. Tap, tap. *The loud sounds from moving shopping carts made me nervous. I was scared of people walking behind me. The music playing over the PA system reminded me of the mortuary music.* Tap, tap. *I forgot what I went there for. I couldn't focus on what to buy. I was gripping Cicero's arm and breaking into a sweat. We went home.*

"What else gives you panic attacks?"

I was crying in bed and put my head on Cicero's chest. The sound of his heartbeat made me jerk my head back and cry even louder. I imagined him being shot in the chest and his heart stopping. Tap, tap.

I have a constant feeling that I am being punished. I wish I was never born.

"Do you have a feeling of doom? Like no matter what happens, only bad things will come?"

Yes.

"That is a common symptom of PTSD. You have PTSD. Of course you do after what has happened. Who wouldn't? You lost your son in a senseless act of violence. You've lost your sense of community. You don't know who to trust because you don't know who did this." She looked into my eyes and held my stare. I looked away.

"Do you feel a sense of shame?"

I didn't respond.

"You said you have trouble looking at people in the eye, and you're looking away now. Do you feel shame?"

"Yes. I feel shame and I don't know why."

I was lying. I *did* know why. My one job as a parent was to raise my children to be happy, healthy adults. My one job was to make sure they had everything they needed before I died. And even if my head told me there was nothing I could have done, that we can only do so much as parents, my heart told me that I failed. I failed him. I should have been there. He should have been with us, looking at wedding sites. *I failed.*

I closed my eyes and called them in. And one by one, they came. Oprah. Maya. Cicero. Julie.

After our first two sessions, Marsha submitted her report for my file:

PSYCHOTHERAPY NOTE

Diagnoses

ACUTE POSTTRAUMATIC STRESS DISORDER - Primary

Precipitating Stress:

Patient states that her 23 year old son was shot and killed in a double shooting two weeks ago. Patient states that she is struggling significantly with the loss, often having intrusive thoughts and images of the violence of patient's son's death. Patient states she was not eating or sleeping the first week and has gotten more of an appetite in the past week. Patient states that she is only able to sleep if she takes low doses of Benadryl and a couple glasses of wine. Patient reports increased alcohol use since his death. Patient is single but good friends with her children's father.

Symptoms Present:

Pati complains of onset and middle insomnia, crying spells, feeling 'numb', withdrawal from affection of others, loss of concentration, low appetite, isolation, anxiety and irritability, intrusive memories, disturbing dreams, physical reactions and avoidance re: the sudden death of her son and loss of interest in ADL [activities of daily living], feeling distant, easily startled.

Grief

Chapter 6

Let It Out

Cora Mendoza was everything I was not.

We were both Filipino Americans. We both grew up in Vallejo. We both had parents who were in real estate. But that's where the similarities ended. She was bubbly and outgoing, while I was shy and reserved. She was athletic and spent her summers working as a lifeguard at the community pool. I was always the last person to be chosen on a team during P.E. class, and was terrified of the water. She exuded confidence, while I was self-conscious. She was a product of a private-school education at an all-girls school. I was public school all the way, often lurking behind bushes on my walk home to avoid a boy named Jay. He'd come up behind me on his bike and for no reason at all start firing closed-fist punches at my arm. Cora would have never stood for that.

And yet we clicked.

I met Cora once when I was in middle school. Our mutual friend, Lisa, brought me to a basketball game at St. Vincent's, the private school she attended. Cora was with the other cheerleaders in their green and white outfits, giggling and scoping out the players. "Let's go say hi," said Lisa. We walked over and she introduced me to each of them, ending with "And this is Cora." She looked me up and down as I began to shrink inside. It wasn't until the summer before my freshman year at UC Davis that I saw Cora again. She and I had enrolled in a summer program at the university. When she said hello I reminded her that we had met years ago, and from there we began a close friendship.

Sophomore year we became roommates in a large, four-bedroom townhome that we shared with five other girls. Everyone had a roommate except for one girl, and Cora and I decided we would share the room on the second floor next to the loft. There were times during that school year when she and I would argue and the loft came in handy as a barrier, but for the most part we had fun taking full advantage of our freedom from our parents and families back in Vallejo.

Cora and I scanned our perfectly coordinated room: two twin beds with simple white wooden frames, each of them pushed up against opposite walls from each other. We bought matching black-and-white bed covers with images of cats—not because we had a shared love of cats, but because they were the only black-and-white covers we could find. Perhaps inspired by the popularity of Patrick Nagel's bold Art Deco prints of the late '80s, we agreed that everything in our room would follow a black, white and red color theme.

Between the beds were our matching white drafting tables with black desk lamps clamped onto the sides. We even set up track lights above the window with red light bulbs.

"It looks so cool!" I said to her, as we hung the last of our clothes in the closet. We had more parties in that townhome than we could count. It wasn't uncommon to find a stranger sleeping in our bathtub the next morning or vomit in the plants outside our front door. It was a wonder the girls found the energy to live together again the following year. I would not be joining them.

After sophomore year we went home for the summer, where I

decided to take classes at a local community college. It was there that I met Ruben. Within six months, we were married and I was pregnant with Robby. Cora and our other roommates stood by me at the altar of St. Basil's church in Vallejo in what would have to be the loudest bridesmaids dresses I could find—hot pink with swirls of organza cascading from their shoulders to the hems. I was 20 and thought Contempo Casuals was the height of fashion. While they continued to live together, I began a family life and finished my last two years of college as a young wife and mother.

I lost touch with the girls after this. I returned to school at Davis in 1991 after Robby was born, but my bag of bottles and diapers seemed out of place at their parties filled with shot glasses and kegs of beer. I took night classes my senior year to accommodate Ruben's work schedule. It was there that I met Audrea Williams. She and I met in Spanish class while I was seven months pregnant with Julie, concealing my swollen belly with Ruben's oversized blazers. We struck up a friendship after we were assigned to the same study group.

"I might not be here the last few weeks of class because of my due date," I said.

"Your what?" she responded.

"My due date . . . for my baby." I unbuttoned my blazer and framed my stomach with my hands, like Vanna White showcasing the winning phrase.

"Girl, I didn't even know you were pregnant!" she squealed.

We were inseparable after that. She attended our family gatherings, playing with Robby, who was barely two years old at the time. We talked for hours about starting our own magazine focused on race relations. We were determined that she—a beautiful, strong African American woman—and I—a shy Filipino American woman who found power in her pen—were going to make a difference in the world.

But before our revolution, I had to give birth to another baby.

Julie was born on February 7, 1993. My water broke just as I was leaving our apartment to take a test on Chaucer's *The Legend of Good Women.*

I asked Cora to be one of her godmothers, along with Margie and Valerie, our other roommates. "Oh, my gosh, of course!" Cora replied, as I knew she would.

Audrea and I kept in touch after graduation and after she got married, but when Ruben and I moved back to Vallejo our calls became fewer and further between, until eventually we lost touch completely. It would be more than two decades before I would reconnect with her.

At 23, I was a wife and a young mother of two. I managed to graduate from UC Davis, but my life was nothing like that of any of my friends. While Ruben and I were settling into family life, Cora had the freedom to move from city to city, job to job, exploring her 20s as any normal twentysomething would do. I kept tabs on her from afar, when she lived in Sacramento, then in Oakland—though between my job and my home life, I wasn't able to see her much. It wasn't until 2000, when I started working at the San Francisco Chronicle, that I got a phone call from her saying that she would be in the city for work and asking if I wanted to meet up for a drink.

It was clear we had both changed since the black, white and red days of our shared room. She had started working at a pharmaceutical company but wasn't completely convinced it was for her, referring to her situation as a "rat race." I was now a journalist with growing kids. We both wanted a little of what the other had—she envied my stability; I, her freedom. It wasn't surprising to me when I got a call from her at the end of 2002 and she casually declared, as only she could, "I'm moving to Hawaii. I quit my job and sold my stuff."

She didn't have a job waiting, a place to live or a plan. She was following her heart, in the form of her boyfriend, who had followed the sun and the waves to Maui. We all expected her to come back after a year or two, consumed by island fever. But she never did, and in 2007 I received her wedding invitation. Her wedding took place on the grounds of a beautiful rustic sugar mill, surrounded by the island's decadent greenery and sounds of the ocean. I watched her exchange vows, with her parents, sisters, brother, nephews and nieces looking on.

What a beautiful family, I thought.

She had been one of my most supportive friends as I was grieving, coordinating with my local friends to set up spa treatments for me, sending me gifts, and checking in on me regularly. When she heard the news about Robby's shooting, she reached out to our other college roommates, booked a flight and was on a plane to be by my side as soon as she possibly could.

After the prayer at the mortuary, she showed up at my house with our other girlfriends, wine bottles in hand. We formed a circle around a table in my loft, refilling our glasses all night and emptying all the bottles. I didn't say much that night; it just helped having them all there. It was past midnight when we decided to turn in.

"Pati, I have something for you," said Cora, handing me a small box. I opened it and found a necklace with two silver discs at the end of it and a dangling crystal. Robby's name was hammered onto the smaller pendant. The larger disc read: *Always in my heart.* "I know Robby's birthstone is a diamond, but I couldn't really afford that," Cora said. "That's what this crystal is for. His birthstone."

I wore the necklace every day after that, holding onto the disc with his name for strength during his funeral and whenever I was overwhelmed with grief.

༄

11:06 p.m.

Pati, I'm sorry it's late and you don't need to respond. I just want you to know I'm having a moment of weakness and my heart is aching for you right now. I hope you're doing better as each day passes. Do you want to talk right now?

Cora's timing was impeccable. I had been crying in bed for hours now, trying to muffle my cries as Cicero slept soundly next to me. He had been spending all his waking hours taking care of me, and I didn't want to disturb him. It was too late to call anyone else. But Cora lived in Hawaii, and it was still early there. I grabbed my phone, slowly crept out from under the covers and headed to Robby's room, where I sat on his bed and called Cora.

"Pati?" she answered. She sat on the phone just listening to me cry, not saying a word. "Just let it out," she said. "I'm here. I'll stay on the phone as long as you need me to. Just let it out."

I finally explained that I had been feeling so abandoned and alone. Aside from Cicero and our immediate family, all our other friends had somewhat retreated—not because they didn't care, but because they didn't know what to do.

"I don't know what it is, but I was just sitting here folding my laundry," she responded. "And I felt this pit in my stomach, like I had to call you, right now."

Cora would get this feeling several times again in the following months, and it was always when I really needed someone.

"We have a connection," I told her. "You always know when to reach out to me."

It was a connection that surprised her as well. "For some reason I can feel your pain," she said. "I haven't lost a child. I am so far from understanding."

Though we were 2,000 miles away from each other, I leaned on her for support. In fact, the support of people from afar proved to be much more "comfortable" than support from people nearby. For many, my physical presence was just too much of a reminder— of my pain and the fact that at any moment, anything can happen.

Chapter 7

I Don't Know What to Say

I stared at the Apple icon on my 21.5-inch monitor waiting to Skype with my colleague from Okinawa. At any moment Katsu's face would appear, and I wasn't sure what my initial expression should be. It was our first Skype call, our first correspondence since Robby died. If I looked the way I felt, he may be uncomfortable. If I smile, he'll wonder how I can be happy after losing my son.

The last time I saw Katsu was during our trip to Tokyo, a month before the tragedy. Katsu returned to his hometown of Okinawa in May 2013, after living in the Bay Area for five years. He and I had gone on several business trips together: Italy, the Philippines, Japan, Indonesia. We had become close friends, and he and Cicero were nurturing their budding bromance.

"Pati-san, I am getting married, and I hope to be great father someday," he told me as we walked along the water at Jack London Square in Oakland one day. I invited him to stay at our house before he left.

That following Saturday, Cicero, Robby and I drove to Berkeley to pick up Katsu at a house he was sharing with several roommates. He came out with a backpack and a childlike grin. He opened the door to the back seat and settled himself in next to Robby. Seated side by side they looked like David and Goliath—Katsu with his slender frame, Robby with his massive shoulders, chest and arms. We drove up the coast to Point Reyes, where we found an oyster shack located between the highway and the ocean. Robby and Katsu waited at one of the wooden tables that lined the roadside while Cicero and I ordered the platters of oysters—raw, barbecued, Rockefeller. We sat in the sun, the ocean waves crashing in the backdrop, with beer and sodas washing down the sweet, briny morsels.

"Wow," Katsu said. "I will miss America."

By the end of Katsu's stay with us, he and Robby agreed that Robby would go to Okinawa one day. He would surf in the ocean just minutes away from Katsu's house, and he would learn about the famous Okinawan diet that was responsible for the population's longevity.

"I'll see you in Okinawa," he said to Robby as they said their goodbyes.

When Julie created the donation page for her brother, I saw that Katsu and Professor Wada from Kyoto were among the first to contribute.

"Pati-san!" Katsu's face appeared on the monitor. His excitement lasted for just seconds before he appeared confused. His smile melted away and gave way to a look of sadness. He didn't know what to do either. I looked past his face and saw the ocean in the background, thinking of Robby surfing those waters.

"I want to thank you," I said, before breaking into tears. "I want to thank you for your donation and being so kind to Robby. He really wanted to visit you one day."

Katsu lowered his head and began to sob. "Pati-san, I don't know what to say. I don't know how to say what I feel in English." For the rest of our conversation, Katsu looked at the camera, speaking Japanese with tears flowing down his face. And though I didn't understand a word he was saying, I understood the love he was sending. It was perhaps one of the most genuine moments I had experienced after Robby's funeral.

⟿

I had changed overnight. Pre-tragedy, I was known among friends and family as the loud, funny one. But it wasn't always that way. Prior to journalism, I was painfully shy. So shy that I woke up in the office of my elementary school after fainting—once while feeling pressured to work out a math problem on the chalkboard, a second time while giving an oral report on how I spent my summer. After that, I was allowed to stay seated while answering any questions that were potentially stress-inducing. After becoming a journalist, I was forced to talk to people. I was invited to give presentations and address crowds. And after journalism, I was giving presentations to national governments and larger audiences. I shed my fear of public speaking, and I often used humor to relate to people and put them at ease. This spilled over to my personal life. I was the friend who liked to make big meals for everyone, invite people over, host out-of-towners. I was the "mother-cousin" of all my cousins, hosting holidays, babysitting, helping with writing projects. The go-to person when someone needed something.

Post-tragedy, I couldn't be that person anymore. I had no jokes left in me, no desire to make any meals. I couldn't focus on filling out simple forms for my insurance, let alone help with any writing projects. My fear of public speaking came back, along with all its debilitating symptoms: dizziness, panic, anxiety. I was a child again. People didn't know how to deal with the changes they saw in me. Those who came every day during the nine-day prayers were nowhere to be seen. There was discomfort in my lingering depression. There was even greater discomfort in the fact that I had lost my son in a tragic way. I found it was often my role to make the other person feel comfortable by forcing a smile or pretending everything was okay. It wasn't. I was put on psychiatric disability and didn't work for nearly four months.

There were friends like Cora and Katsu who didn't recoil and run from my pain but instead took my hand, sat with me, stayed on the phone with me and allowed me to just grieve.

They were open, brave . . . and rare.

In general, friends and family fell in one of the following categories: 1) People who didn't know what to say and acted like the tragedy never happened (*Oh, you look great, have you lost weight?*); 2) People who felt they had to say something, not realizing their words were insensitive or intrusive (*So what happened? Where was he shot?*); 3) People who compared their pain with mine (*Well, you know, I lost my grandmother and that was really hard on me.*); 4) People who stayed away completely.

I resented all of them, until I asked myself how I would feel and what I would do in their shoes. For some people I was a walking ice pick, jabbing at their own open wounds and re-injuring those that were long healed and forgotten. So they avoided me altogether.

This was something that still stung with Richard. During my first and only therapy session with him, he did little to hide his bitterness. "People will say to you, 'I can't imagine what it feels like to lose a child.' When all they're really saying is, 'I don't want to imagine it. Better you than me.'"

I immediately thought of all the times I had said that to someone, but I never meant it the way he had come to interpret it. This allowed me to understand that perhaps I was misinterpreting what people were saying to me. Because honestly, when you are hurting and you don't know who it is that caused the pain, you just need someone to lash out at. And I spared no one.

Nothing incensed me more than when someone would try to rationalize Robby's death.

They would speak with certainty on why or how this could happen—as if there were any justifications for it. People projected their need to make sense of things onto me by saying that this was what God wanted, or that it was part of his plan. But I did not share in this source of comfort. My son did not die of natural causes or old age. His was a tragic death for which there were no words—no spiritual justification—that made it okay for him to die at the hands of another person at the age of 23.

My friend Eva Konigsberg, whom both Katsu and I worked with at Global Footprint Network, had been listening patiently as I went down the list of things people had said to me that were offensive and/or insensitive. "What a bitch," she'd blurt out in a show of support. "Horrible person." She tilted her head and looked at me with her intense hazel eyes after I had exhausted my examples, and with the most tender of tones said, "Listen. My friend Paula died after a horrible battle with cancer. She was young, beautiful, lively, vivacious, tried all kinds of weird food diets to beat the cancer, but in the end it got her. I saw her mother at the funeral. I didn't know what to say. So I figured I'd say to her what my aunt said to me when my mom died. I hugged Paula's mother and said, 'Have faith.' Her mother stopped suddenly, put her hands on my shoulder and looked me squarely in the eyes. She said, 'I just buried my third child. What am I supposed to have faith in?'

"I felt awful. I mean, geez, people don't know what the fuck to say," Eva told me. "But you have to tell yourself that everyone wants to help. They just don't know how."

She was right. Even those of us in the inner circle—Ruben, Cicero, Julie, Robby's grandparents—didn't know how to speak to one another. I was lashing out at Cicero, accusing him of not caring, not understanding how I felt. Even though he was grieving himself. We treated Julie with velvet gloves, not wanting to expose her to anything about the investigation or show her how much we were truly suffering. But in doing so she felt she had to be strong for us, concealing her grief as well. Ruben spent every day at the cemetery, spending hours by Robby's grave. He had stopped answering phone calls and leaving his house, other than to go to the cemetery.

But our grief was not in sync. While one person may have found momentary strength, another would be experiencing anger or depression. We were all over the place, yet we were all we had because nobody understood what we were going through. We, too, didn't know what the fuck to say, to each other or anyone else. And then one day, just as he had done for me when I was a child, Mr. Rogers comforted and educated me with his words. I had been walking around my local Barnes & Noble bookstore looking for more books on the afterlife when I spotted this:

> *People have said, 'Don't cry' to other people for years and years, and all it has ever meant is, 'I'm too uncomfortable when you show your feelings. Don't cry.' I'd rather have them say, 'Go ahead and cry. I'm here to be with you."*
> —*Fred Rogers,* The World According to Mister Rogers

Chapter 8

I Feel Your Pain

Less than one week after Robby was killed, another young man was brutally shot down in Vallejo. I would have never known about it had it not been the topic of conversation among many who attended one of the rosary prayers. I caught hushed snippets as I walked through the house.

He had a truck, too . . .

So close to where it happened . . .

Might be related?

I searched the Internet that night for "Vallejo" and "shooting" and found an article on the San Francisco Chronicle's website written by Henry K. Lee, a former colleague who covered local crime, including high-profile stories, such as the Laci and Scott Peterson case. On the night Robby was killed, Henry reached out to me and Cicero, who was also a former reporter at the Chronicle, and asked for a quote. I sent him something back, though I don't remember what it was now. I never read his article, but I suppose it was similar to the one I found on this young man's incident:

Thursday, September 25, 2014

Man shot in Vallejo's second homicide this week

By Henry K. Lee

A man died after he was shot in his truck in Vallejo, the second homicide in the city this week, police said Thursday.

The latest shooting was discovered about 9:20 p.m. Wednesday when officers found the victim in his truck at Admiral Callaghan Lane and Columbus Parkway, said police Sgt. Joe Iacono.

The man had been shot numerous times and died at a hospital. His name has not been released.

The shooting happened two miles from where Robby Poblete, 23, of Vallejo was shot and killed on Admiral Callaghan Lane about 5:25 p.m. Sunday.

Poblete was the son of former San Francisco Chronicle writer and editor Pati Poblete.

No arrests have been made in the slayings. It was not known if the two killings were related.

I continued to check the updates on the case until his name was released because I wanted desperately to reach out to his mother. I wanted her to know she wasn't alone—or maybe it was me who needed a mother I could relate to. Grief from the loss of a child can't be comforted by stories of how others lost a parent, spouse or friend to illness or a car accident. It's a different type of grief, not to say it is any more or less painful. But it's a grief that begs for survivors to come together and share in the trauma of losing a child at the hands of another person.

Parent of a homicide victim. Mother who lost her son to gun violence.

That was me now, and I wanted to find others like me. Before Robby's death, I saw news stories about shootings all the time, but now I was hyper-sensitive. Anything related to guns and shooting deaths made me immediately think of the victims' mothers and those of the shooters. Being the parent of a murder victim was excruciatingly painful, but being the parent of a murderer, I simply could not fathom. There were so many stories following Robby's death, not just from Vallejo, but across the nation. I felt the despair of every mother losing her child to gun violence. And the weight was becoming unbearable.

A little over a month after Robby was killed, 15-year-old Jaylen Fryberg texted five other students in Marysville, Washington, to meet him at the school cafeteria, including two of his cousins and three friends. He then used a .40-caliber Beretta and shot all five of them, killing four before turning the gun on himself.

A month after this incident, the news was flooded with the story of Tamir Rice, a 12-year-old African American boy who was shot and killed by a Cleveland police officer. Rice had been carrying a toy gun. The young boy died from a "gunshot wound of torso with injuries of major vessel, intestines and pelvis," according to an autopsy report released by the Cuyahoga County Medical Examiner. His death was ruled a homicide.

And the list went on and on. These news reports did not plant a seed of activism in me—in fact, they had an opposite effect. The stories were inescapable, serving as a constant reminder that the issue was too big. The challenge too overwhelming. The pain too widespread. With every news story I saw on a shooting death, I knew that somewhere there was a mother crying out for her child.

After the name of the homicide victim in Vallejo was released, I searched for his mother on Facebook and sent her a private message telling her that my son was killed, too, not far from her own. I told her that I hoped her family, friends and the community would provide her with strength and support as they had done for me. I told her I was there for her, even if we didn't know each other, and that I was sending all my love her way. I didn't tell her I was praying for her, that her son was in a better place or that it was

God's will. She didn't respond, but I saw my message was marked as "read," and I hoped my words were some source of comfort to her.

I continued to reach out to other mothers—all of whom were strangers. Because they had lost their children to gun violence, I felt they understood me better than any of my closest friends and relatives ever could. And I could understand them.

My therapist recommended several support groups, including The Compassionate Friends, whose mission was to provide "highly personal comfort, hope, and support to every family experiencing the death of a son or a daughter, a brother or a sister, or a grand-child, and [help] others better assist the grieving family."

There was the National Organization of Parents of Murdered Children (POMC), whose mission was "to provide support and assistance to all survivors of homicide victims while working to create a world free of murder."

There were groups for people who suffered from PTSD. Another one for panic attacks. I wasn't ready for any of these groups. I was okay with reaching out to parents individually, but I wasn't ready to group myself as one of them. It made it too real—and complicated.

There were days when I would wake up motivated to take action. Pick myself up, take a walk and play an active role in my healing. Turn my tragedy into something that could help others—*advocacy for gun reform? A foundation in Robby's name?* And then just like that, I'd ask myself, "What's the point?"

Take a stand/stay in bed. Let your voice be heard/heal in silence. Live your life/get through the day. These were choices that ran through my head every day, and more often than not, I chose the latter. For me to weigh in on the gun debate would have been like flicking a speck of dust on a wildfire.

It had been two years since the tragic shooting at Sandy Hook

Elementary School in Newtown, Connecticut. Two years since a troubled 20-year-old shot and killed his mother in their home before heading to the school and fatally shooting 20 children, all between the ages of six and seven, as well as six adult staff members. I watched President Barack Obama deliver a tearful speech from the Briefing Room on December 12, 2012, the same day as the mass shooting. He stood behind a podium marked with the presidential seal in his tailored black suit and silver, striped tie, with an American flag pinned on his left lapel. He was flanked by the flag of the president of the United States on his left and the American flag to his right; behind him, the large oval logo of the White House. But on this day, all the pomp and circumstance of the office he held couldn't mask the fact that he was simply a parent. A parent who may not have lost a child, but who was imagining what it would be like to lose one in such a brutal way. Struggling from one sentence to the next and stopping to wipe his tears, he said:

We've endured too many of these tragedies in the past few years. And each time I learn the news I react not as a resident, but as anybody else would—as a parent. And that was especially true today. I know there's not a parent in America who doesn't feel the same overwhelming grief that I do.

Nine days later, the National Rifle Association held its own press conference. After expressing his "horror, outrage, grief and earnest prayer for the families of Newtown, Connecticut," NRA Executive Vice President Wayne LaPierre offered what he believed could have prevented the school shooting and could prevent anything like it from ever happening again: guns in schools.

Because for all the noise and anger directed at us over the past week, no one—nobody—has addressed the most important, pressing and immediate question we face: How do we protect our children right now, starting today, in a way that we know works?"

The only way to answer that question is to face up to the truth.

Politicians pass laws for gun-free school zones. They issue press releases bragging about them. They post signs advertising them.

And in so doing, they tell every insane killer in America that schools are their safest place to inflict maximum mayhem with minimum risk.

Once again, even after 20 innocent children were gunned down, nothing happened. I watched and heard people who opposed any type of gun reform, including some friends and family, preach the sanctity of the Second Amendment, with no seeming interest in the fact that gun *reform* didn't equate to gun *ban*. How would they feel, I wondered, if one of those children killed were one of their own?

My career—though varied in job titles and industries—was held together by one common thread: hope.

I entered each position knowing that if I did my job well, I would play a part in creating a better future: improving the lives of millions of foster care children through writing editorials; helping save and improve lives of cancer patients as a media advocacy director for the American Cancer Society; helping address climate change and other environmental crises by working with national governments and intergovernmental agencies.

This last job was what fascinated Robby the most and one of the main reasons that prompted him to get his passport. He wanted to join me on my trips and learn about other cultures, learn about my work and, yes, practice yoga in the ashrams throughout India.

So when Robby died, many people expected me to channel my grief into what I knew: advocacy. But there was no hope and no fight left in me. This was a battle I didn't think I could ever help win. If the faces of 20 rosy-cheeked children plastered in news magazines and on TV channels around the nation couldn't move our country to change, then what was the death of my 23-year-old son in a formerly bankrupt city going to do? What little energy

I had left I had to preserve for Julie. I was still a mother to one living child.

I thought of starting a foundation to honor Robby's love for cycling. I would call it "Robby's Riders" and distribute bicycles to children in different countries who had no way of getting to school. Every year on his birthday, we would hold Robby's Ride, where every child with a donated bike would ride together to raise money for bicycles for other children. I thought of where the bikes would be stored, how we could distribute them, what foundations to approach for funding. I thought of a logo, where the two "B's" in Robby's name would serve as the wheels of a bicycle. But how could I start a foundation when I couldn't get out of bed? It was like watching fruit blossom and ripen on the vine, only to let it rot and fall to the ground. My moods were volatile, and the last thing I wanted to do was to commit myself to a routine by joining a support group or starting anything I couldn't finish.

Medication. There was medication—for anxiety, for sleeplessness, for depression. I told Marsha I didn't want to take any of it. "There is no pill that can help me get over my son's death," I said. "There is no pill that can fix that or bring him back."

"Yes," she responded. "But you cannot continue functioning with three hours of sleep, and pretty soon you will have to return to work." Marsha recommended I start with low doses to help me sleep.

PSYCHOTHERAPY NOTE

Treatment Plan/Assessment: Woman with acute Post Traumatic Stress Disorder, terrible grief.

Reviewed medication options including SSRIs, prazosin, trazodone, benzodiazepines, low-dose atypical antipsychotics. Recommended trial of prazosin; declines at this time. Most comfortable with low dose lorazepam (1 mg 1/2-1 bid prn) in addition to trazodone which may be increased to 100 mg hs. In addition to other benefits/risks/alternatives (including no medication), I discussed dependency, abuse, motor impairment (i.e. exercise caution with driving and other tasks), to never mix alcohol with this medication and to be cautious of use in combination with other sedating medications. The patient expressed understanding and voluntarily consents.

I never even made it to the pharmacy to pick up the medications. I agreed several times over the course of therapy to take medications to help me sleep, ease my anxiety or smooth out the sharp edges of my depression. "Yes," I'd say, agreeing that something had to be done. She'd call in the prescriptions to my local pharmacy, where the pills varying in shape, size and strength sat in their amber-colored bottles. And there they would remain, unclaimed, unopened, unconsumed. Not because I had any moral opposition to psychiatric drugs, but because I knew I was vulnerable. If anything helped numb my pain, if anything helped me out of the nightmare, I was afraid I would need it for the rest of my life. Because who would willingly crawl back into darkness once they've found the escape route?

"Then you need to find a way to cope with your grief, because you are in depression. Are you having suicidal thoughts?" she asked.

No, but I wish I was never born.

"And what do you think Robby would want you to do?"

He would want me to live.

Pathway

Chapter 9

Follow Me

The parking lot near the freeway off-ramp was mostly empty when I pulled in that Sunday morning. The sun was already out, but the air remained brisk. I scanned the parking lot as I pulled into an empty space, but I didn't see anyone around. Water bottle, check. Sunglasses and gym towel, check. I gathered the items and stuffed them into the small canvas bag that would sit underneath the seat of my bicycle. I reached behind my driver's seat for my bike helmet and began adjusting the straps under my chin.

"Hey, Mom!" I turned around to see Robby riding toward me in full cycling gear: black Lycra cycling bib, fitted cycling hat with its flipped-up bill. His outfit reminded me of the guy in the Tae Bo exercise videos.

"Oh, Robby!" I said, laughing.

"What?" he said, riding in circles around me.

"Where did you get that outfit?"

"It's awesome!" he answered, laughing along with me.

It was Mother's Day, 2013, and his gift to me was a long bike ride together. I met him here, near Ruben's house, and carved out the whole day for our ride. "Where are we going?" I asked.

"Just follow me," he said. I grabbed the rest of my gear, unlocked my bike from the rack and set out to follow him, but he had already taken off.

"Over here!" he yelled. He took the lead, heading into the bike lane on the street, and looking back to check on me every 10 minutes or so. "You okay?" he'd ask.

"Yes, I'll ring my bell if I need anything," I responded.

He came to a stop in front of a steep concrete on-ramp, leading to a long pedestrian overpass that would take us into the neighboring city. "Want me to bring my bike up and then come down and get yours?" he asked.

"I can do it," I replied, semi-convincingly. He then took both bicycles, one in each hand, hoisted them over his shoulders, and proceeded to climb up as if he were holding two loaves of bread. His Herculean strength always amazed me.

When we reached the other side, he warned me that we would have to ride alongside traffic. "Just follow me, k?" I didn't know where he was taking me, but I said okay and proceeded to follow him. Cars whisked by us, but I kept my eyes focused on the back of Robby's bike.

He led me through the downtown area of Fairfield, California, lined with old buildings housing new businesses. We passed city hall, the courthouse, a patch of grass where the farmers market was held every Thursday. He pointed out the bike shop where he helped Cicero pick out the bike I was now riding. The Mediterranean market where he bought spices. "They have the best shawarmas!" he yelled, pointing to the hole-in-the-wall to his left.

We rode along the main road until he motioned to cross the street after we went under an overpass. I had never been to this part of town and I had no idea where we were going. I followed him as he crossed, riding onto the sidewalk and between two metal poles. Suddenly we were on a seemingly hidden bike trail surrounded by trees and shrubs, riding adjacent to the freeway, though you would never know it because it was well enclosed.

"This is the trail I use to ride to work sometimes," he said. We followed along the trail, passing through open fields filled with nothing but grass and wildflowers. We rode through farms with stands selling stone fruits, melons and corn.

We had been riding for nearly two hours when we came across a structure that looked like a house in a fairytale—white and pink exterior with flowers painted on its wooden shutters. A sign read: *Fresh pies and honey.*

I rang my bike bell, catching Robby's attention. "Let's go in there!" I yelled.

He turned his bike around, heading toward the Hansel and Gretel-looking house. We went in, scanning the different pies, assortment of old-fashioned candies and vintage kitsch. We each bought a slice—one apple, one strawberry rhubarb—and sat on the wicker seats on the porch, keeping an eye on our unlocked bikes.

"Where to next?" I asked.

"I'm just biking," he said. "It's better that way. You don't always have to know where you're going."

We hopped on our bikes afterward, heading back to the main country road. I tried adjusting my gears as we approached an incline. Without looking back, Robby turned his bike around, came up behind me and placed his hand on my back, pushing me forward for the length of the hill. "C'mon, Mom," he said. "I got you."

We stopped a few times, taking pictures of grazing horses and different pastoral scenes.

"Can we stop real quick?" I'd ask.

"Go ahead," he'd respond, riding in circles until I'd captured whatever it was I wanted to capture.

It was late afternoon when we reached an old wooden shed that had been converted into a deli and coffeehouse. Other than the slices of pie, we hadn't eaten all day. We looked at each other and knew instinctively that we would be making the stop. The wooden stairs and porch creaked as we walked on them. Old chairs lined the front of the wraparound porch. I pictured us whittling pieces of wood on those chairs, spitting tobacco from the sides of our mouths. That's how deep in the countryside we were. We pulled the swinging door open, walking into the cozy space. The menu listed off smoothies, sandwiches, espresso and lattes. At the far end was an assortment of cold drinks. Our water bottles had run dry hours ago and we were parched.

"I just want a smoothie," said Robby. He would go through periods like this—extreme biking/surfing/surfing coupled with a strict diet regimen.

"Fine with me, I want food," I replied.

We took our orders out onto the porch overlooking the field across from us. It was the most time we had spent together in a long time.

"What's the longest you've ever ridden?" I asked. He told me he had biked from Vallejo to Oakland, which was a 45-minute drive by freeway. "Isn't that dangerous?" I asked.

"No, it's fun!" he said, as if I was being ridiculous.

"Well, I'm not ready for that kind of ride. I think I'm ready to head back soon."

He nodded his head, finishing his smoothie in less than three gulps. We sat for a while afterward, sharing plans about the new house we were about to move into. He said he might be staying with his dad more, depending on a job he was looking into, but he would be home on the weekends. He had ideas about his room. He wanted to build shelves and make mandalas out of wood, which he would hang on the wall above his bed. Maybe he'd build his own bed frame. I asked him about his plans beyond his room, his plans for his life.

"I want to travel someday," he said. "I want to see the places you've seen. And I want to live on a boat." How he would financially support those plans was still unknown, but he knew that's what he wanted.

He had been working at a county-run organization for more than a year now, serving as one of the instructors at the facility that served 75 adults with developmental disabilities. His job included overseeing and assisting with a variety of community, job training and classroom activities, including taking the adults on field trips and to various jobs around the Bay Area.

He was learning a lot about patience, understanding and compassion, but I knew this was not what he wanted for a career. Luckily, he said, he applied for a temporary job at his dad's work. "If I get in, maybe they'll hire me full time," he said. The idea of building things and working with his hands excited him.

"I'm sure you'll get a call soon," I said.

When it was my turn to share, I told him that Cicero and I wanted to get married sometime soon, and since my dad passed away in 2000, I wanted him to walk me down the aisle. He smiled. "When is that going to be?" he asked, clearly calculating how much time he had to reach his goal weight.

"I'm not sure yet, but hopefully this year or next."

"Okay, well, let me know when you know the date."

We got back on our bikes, hoping to get back to my car before it went dark. I followed him along the same path, through the fields, through the covered bike path, back downtown and over the pedestrian overpass. It was just dusk when our ride ended, the sky painted in hues of pink and orange.

"Thanks, Son," I said, taking my helmet off.

"I hope you liked your day," he replied. "I hope it was a good Mother's Day."

He gave me a kiss on the cheek and a hug before he headed back to Ruben's house, just a few blocks away. I watched him ride away in his comical outfit, knowing that I would always remember the Mother's Day that he shared his passion of cycling with me, a gift that required no money, no gift wrapping, and yet brought me so much pure joy.

Chapter 10

His Books

It was past 10:00 p.m. and the piercing sounds still hadn't ceased. It was an alternating cacophony consisting of a power drill, hammering and inexplicable banging. I took a deep breath, got out of bed and headed down the hall.

"Robby!" I yelled, knocking on his door. "It's late! Can you finish that tomorrow?"

"But I'm almost done. Come in and look."

I opened his door to see him standing in the middle of a whole bedroom set he just built out of planks of pine and nails he bought at Home Depot earlier that day. I'd had my doubts. He had never built a bed frame before, or any kind of furniture for that matter. But here he was, power drill in hand and a look of satisfaction.

The frame was built for a queen-size mattress, with an elevated shelf attached to the headboard. To the left of the bed was a nightstand he created with the leftover materials.

"Pretty cool, huh? I'm going to put all my books right here," he said, pointing to the shelf.

"How did you do this?" I asked, pleasantly, if not shockingly, surprised.

"Told you I could," was all he said.

Over the next weeks, the shelf filled up with a growing pile of books on Buddhism, meditation, yoga, philosophy, Rumi, Nietzsche, the Dalai Lama.

After my last session with Marsha I went into his room, sat on his bed, remembering that day. I began going through his pile of books, left untouched since the last day he was home. I scanned some of the titles:

How to Practice: The Way to a Meaningful Life
Living Buddha, Living Christ
The Self Beyond Itself
Light on Life
The Seven Spiritual Laws of Yoga
Science of Being and Art of Living
Phenomenology of Spirit
Autobiography of a Yogi
The Essence of the Bhagavad Gita
Diary of Saint Maria: Divine Mercy in My Soul
How to Be a Surfer
It's All About the Bike

I picked up *Living Buddha, Living Christ,* by the Vietnamese monk, Zen master and poet Thich Nhat Hanh. The spine was worn; its pages were dog-eared. I began to read, hoping to understand the world that Robby was living in. I sat in his room the rest of that day, reading.

Our capacity to make peace with another person and with the world depends very much on our capacity to make peace with ourselves.

I read about mindfulness, about forgiveness, about suffering—not as a rite of passage, but as an option that we, as humans, often inflict upon ourselves. For the first time, I was reading that suffering was not something inevitable, required or honorable. It was *avoidable.* Pain, like love, was inescapable, but prolonged suffering did not have to be.

I wanted to read more. I found the last book Robby gave me as a Christmas gift, which had been sitting on a stack of other books on my nightstand, *The Art of Happiness in a Troubled World* by His Holiness the Dalai Lama and Howard C. Cutler, M.D. Its words and messages moved me deeply and addressed many things I had been wrestling with: *Is it possible to be truly happy when social problems invariably impact our personal happiness? In seeking happiness do we choose the path of inner development or social change?*

Through his books, I felt as though Robby had sprinkled bread crumbs, gently easing me out of the darkness and onto a path toward healing. All I had to do was follow his trail.

I believe the very purpose of our life is to seek happiness. Whether one believes in religion or not, whether one believes in that religion or this religion, we are all seeking something better in life. So, I think, the very motion of our life is towards happiness...

I then started reading his books on ashtanga and vinyasa yoga, which he practiced. Amber, his yoga instructor, sent me a private message on Facebook shortly after Robby died to let me know how sorry she was, and how she loved having him in her classes. I took Robby's yoga mat from his room at Ruben's house and registered for classes at the same yoga studio that Robby had been going to. I walked up the stairs of the two-story building to the small studio. I arrived 15 minutes early, hoping to get a chance to speak with Amber and learn more about her time with Robby. I was the first one there.

I looked around the hot studio with its mirrored walls and hardwood floors. I took Robby's mat out of the yoga bag he bought and unrolled it onto the cool, smooth floor. It had been a while since it had been used, so it continued to roll back. I pressed the corners and laid my body flat on the mat, stretching out my arms and legs to each corner. I looked up at the ceiling, then closed my eyes. I could smell him. Robby's scent, his hair, his skin, his cologne, his sweat, it was still there on the mat. I felt the tears coming.

You're with me, I thought.

"Pati?"

I opened my eyes and saw a petite woman with short brown hair and friendly eyes standing over me. I sat up, wiping my eyes.

"Amber?"

She gave me a warm, lingering hug. "Robby always gave the best hugs," she said. "Big bear hugs. I'm so glad you're here."

As she began to prepare, the class started filling up. I couldn't imagine it. My big Robby doing the downward-facing dog and tree pose with this group of people—a giant in a room of waifs. How did he ever get his body to do the same things that these women, less than half his size, were doing? I could barely keep up.

I started going to class regularly, Robby's yoga mat in tow, feeling my anxiety and panic start to subside. I slowly began regaining strength in my arms and legs and throughout my body, which had become soft and frail from months of being secluded and sedentary. My breathing became more measured and intentional, grounding me and helping me cope with my stress.

Close your eyes and relax your body, starting from the top of your head, to your ears, to your tongue, to your neck, down your arms and to your fingertips . . .

At the end of each session, Amber would gently strike the rim of a small bronze Tibetan singing bowl, causing it to vibrate and produce a long, steady tone.

Gently move your fingers and toes.

Inhale and stretch your arms back behind you.

Exhale and bring your knees to your chest and roll over to the right side.

Come up to a seated position and bring your hands to your heart in a prayer position.

We placed our palms together, following her gentle motions.

Bring your hands to your forehead as a reminder of right thoughts.

Bring your hands to your lips as a reminder of right speech.

Bring your hands to your heart as a reminder of right intentions.

We then let out a communal "Om" and bowed to say our final "Namaste."

The first time I came to her class, the extended "Om" sound sent electricity through my body, like a defibrillator shocking me back to life. That day we were a group of fewer than 10 women, but the sound we produced together was loud, powerful and in perfect harmony. I understood why Robby came here, how it gave him peace. Even if his ability to do any of the poses will forever remain a mystery to me.

Chapter 11

Planting Seeds

When we moved into our new home in Fairfield, our backyard was nothing but a small rectangular patch of dirt enclosed by a fence made of unstained pine. It was so unremarkable and uninspiring that we barely gave any thought to it. The only sign of progress was a kidney-shaped cement patio that Cicero and I had hired a contractor to put in a few months after we moved in. I then bought a few small trees and planted them in halved wine barrels I bought on sale at a local nursery. "You should plant flowers," Robby said. "They'll add color."

Several months after Robby died, I began planting those flowers. I started with his favorites, hibiscus and alstroemeria. And then I couldn't stop. I bought other seedlings—roses, peonies, snapdragons, lilies, daffodils, marigolds, fruit trees, vegetables, climbing vines, succulents—and slowly began creating a garden. I went to the nursery so often that the cashiers knew me and asked if I wanted to open an account. Nurturing the plants and watching them grow had a calming, healing effect on me.

I had a suspicion that gardening had become more than a hobby when, after an afternoon of especially strong winds, I went outside to see my tomato plant toppled over. Many of its branches had snapped and dozens of green cherry tomatoes were scattered on the ground. The plant was completely uprooted from its wine-barrel planter. I struggled to get the plant upright, wrestling with the broken limbs and trying desperately to salvage what was left. Until finally I gave up and cried—actually *cried*. I fell to my knees and sobbed in front of the tomato plant, apologizing to it for failing to keep it alive. It wasn't until I heard voices in my neighbor's yard that I realized how insane I must have sounded.

Obviously, I was working out some issues.

But every morning I would sit with my coffee, then rise to stop by each plant to gauge its progress, nursing each wilting branch or leaf back to health and delicately trimming any signs of decay. In the spring, the dormant brown twigs came alive with budding, yellow-green leaves and blossoms in every color imaginable. In the corner, climbing up a trellis, was a rosebush I planted filled with clusters of snow-white blooms. At the top I placed a sign: *Robby's Roses*.

I placed a statue of a meditating Buddha beneath the shade of a lemon tree and between two climbing beanstalks. In the early mornings, I would stand under the shadow of the jasmine vine, which barely reached my waist when I bought it. Now, it climbed up and over our arbor, emanating the sweetest, most delicate perfume from its ivory, star-shaped flowers. I'd wait for the hummingbirds that often came at this time to dip their beaks into the yellow trumpet flowers and fragrant lavender salvia, getting their fill of nectar. There they would hover until they found a sturdy branch to perch on. At the center of our arbor I placed a simple piece of driftwood with one word: *Serenity*.

Gardening was just my first step in seeking healing through nature. Shortly after I began gardening, Cicero and I started going on long hikes. We started at Muir Woods in Mill Valley, protected by its battalion of giant redwood trees. We spent hours hiking its trails, inhaling the fresh, crisp air and looking up to the treetops that seemingly poked at the clouds. Every weekend we explored a different trail, each one giving us a different vantage point of the Bay Area, different landscapes, different challenges. I scaled the steep trails, my legs burning and my temples dripping with sweat, feeling as if I was fighting my way back.

Being in nature had a profound effect on me. It reminded me how small we are in the context of the universe, while at the same time showing me that we are all part of the same ecosystem, part of this life, each one dependent on the other.

It was during this time that Cora introduced me to someone named Alex Leikermoser, a "wellness coach and lifestyle mentor," who was known among those who worked with her to have a unique and playful approach to inspiring people—from managing weight to reducing stress to cultivating a positive mindset. I began her seven-day online rainbow cleanse, which involved preparing vegetarian, preferably raw, foods each day that followed a color theme. Each color would correlate with a chakra, which we would focus on for that day.

For example, Day One of the cleanse was red. On that day I made a strawberry smoothie for breakfast, beet salad for lunch and a red Swiss chard soup with lentils for dinner. The root chakra for red is located at the bottom of the spine and its meaning is "redemption, courage, cleansing and sacrifice."

For each day we were given a meditation, affirmation and yoga pose to practice. This continued for seven days: red, orange, yellow, green, blue, purple and, finally, white/gold. It was way outside my comfort zone, but it was right in line with something Robby would have tried. I was surprised that it reignited my passion for cooking again, but in a different way. I found it exciting going to the local farmers market looking for all orange, or all purple, fruits and vegetables, then finding a way to prepare them. The exercise opened my eyes to our world's vibrant color palette, which I never truly appreciated until these color-coded treasure hunts. In addition to that, I was becoming healthier and stronger because of it. When it came time for yellow, I happily harvested the bright zucchini blossoms and yellow squash in my backyard, sautéing them lightly and topping them off with fresh basil from my herb garden. I wished I could have shared the experience with Robby.

But even if such sweet moments were tinged with sadness, I knew I was finding my way back to life—with Robby leading the way.

Chapter 12

Shasta Abbey

Robby was anxious to see the layout of our new house, so he accompanied us for the walk-through with the builders. It was located in a development that cut across a stretch of land surrounded by verdant, rolling hills. The engineer who met with us led us through each room, explaining the pipes, the electrical wiring, switches, appliances, sprinkler system, and where the extra buckets of touch-up paint were. At the end of the walk-through, he left us to ourselves as we went through the house discussing what would go where. We found Robby with his eyes closed sitting cross-legged in one of the bedrooms, with his elbows on his knees. I thought maybe he was taking a nap, so I left him there until we were ready to go. He came downstairs shortly afterward, meeting us in the kitchen.

"I want that room," he said, referring to the bedroom he had been sitting in.

The room sat right above the garage with one large window and a series of small, square windows that offered a panoramic view of the open, pastoral setting that encircled our neighborhood. The land across the street was private, and we were assured there would be no future construction there. Sometimes the verdant slopes

were sprinkled with grazing cows, and it felt like we were somewhere in Ireland or a remote English countryside.

"I like the view, and when I meditated in there I had a good
feeling," Robby explained.

That was the first time I heard of him meditating. It came up
again several times afterward—when he felt stress, or when he
came across someone who irritated or upset him. He would go to
his room and sit in his meditation pose and emerge calmer, more
reflective. When Julie would come home upset, he would advise
her to follow the practice: *You just have to be still and free your
mind*, he'd say.

I didn't get it.

After reading Robby's books on meditation, I searched the
Internet for Buddhist retreats. Shasta Abbey was a Buddhist
monastery in the Soto Zen tradition. It was described as a training monastery for Buddhist monks, male and female, and a place
of practice for lay Buddhists and interested visitors. It offered
retreats, ceremonies, teaching and spiritual counseling, as well as
the opportunity to train within a monastic schedule. But before
you could take advantage of the monastery's full menu of offer-
ings, you had to first go through the Introductory Retreat. The
description read:

> *Introductory Retreats begin to provide some answers
> to the questions that bring us to Buddhist practice.
> These retreats offer guests new to Shasta Abbey an
> introduction to the Serene Reflection (Soto Zen) prac-
> tice in a monastic setting. They provide down-to-earth
> suggestions for taking this practice into one's daily*

life outside the monastery gates. Within the monastic schedule, and in silence as much as possible, Introductory Retreats offer meditation instruction, short periods of seated meditation, Dharma talks and informal discussions with time for your questions. There is also the opportunity for private spiritual counseling.

I needed *Buddhism and Meditation for Dummies*, and this was the closest thing I could find.

The abbey was located on 16 acres of forest in Mount Shasta, about a four-hour drive from our house, nearing the Oregon border. I registered both Cicero and myself, just in case my anxiety would prevent me from going through the three full days. He agreed without hesitation, seeking his own form of comfort from all the pain and confusion at the time. He was assigned his own room, across the common room and down the corridor where the men were separated into their own wing.

It was still dark out when the sound of the bell echoed through the guest rooms of the Shasta Abbey Buddhist Monastery the morning after we arrived. I opened my eyes, my blurry vision coming into focus on the scarf I placed over the lampshade to dim the light. We weren't allowed to keep the lights on after a certain time, but I still couldn't sleep in the dark. So I threw my scarf over the shade and stayed up reading a book about forgiveness until 2:00 a.m. But now I was groggy and didn't want to get out of bed.

The bell continued to ding at faster intervals now, signifying it was time to meet at Buddha Hall for our morning meditation. I looked over at the clock: 5:00 a.m. Three hours of sleep. I peeled back the wool blankets, forced myself out of the twin bed, placed my feet on the ground and headed out the door toward the common bathroom where several women were already brushing their teeth and washing the sleep from their eyes. We greeted each other with gentle nods and subdued smiles. We were asked to remain in silence, aside from the scheduled dharma talks where we were allowed to ask questions and engage in discussions.

Cicero and I met in the common room where people were sipping hot tea before heading out into the pre-dawn snow. There were about 25 people in our group. The monastery was shaped like an "L," with the guest rooms on one end and the temple at the other. A narrow, covered cloister connected all the buildings, from the guestrooms to the kitchen, to the dining area, to the private sleeping quarters for the 26-plus monks who lived and taught at the monastery. Some structures stood apart from the main facility, such as the woodshop where monks built and repaired their own furniture, fences and gardening borders, among other things. There was a potting shed and a greenhouse, as well as a sewing room.

We walked in silence out the door, into the cold and along the path. White puffs swirled and dissipated around us as our warm breath converged with the crisp mountain air. At the end of the trail, we turned left and took several creaky wooden steps up to the temple. From here we had a pine-tree-framed view of Mount Shasta, now capped with fresh snow.

Before entering Buddha Hall, we removed our warm jackets, hats, scarves, gloves and shoes. We lined up in front of an old wooden cabinet where meditation and booster cushions were stored. Upon entering, we turned toward the giant statue of the Buddha, placed our palms together in prayer hands and bowed to show respect to the Buddha. This ritual was called *gassho,* which in Japanese literally means "palms of the hands placed together."

The large room was dark, and all I could make out were outlines of people, finding open spots on the floor, each facing the wall to meditate for the next 50 minutes—20 minutes' seated medi-tation, 10 minutes' walking meditation, then 20 minutes' seated meditation. I found a space on the opposite side of the entrance, lifting my hips from side to side on the cushion to find a comfortable position. I placed my elbows on my thighs, then, as we were instructed, I rested my right hand in my lap with my palm facing upward and placed my left hand on top of my right palm. The tips of my thumbs touched lightly to form an oval.

While most people close their eyes during meditation, this practice called for us to merely "soften" our eyes and lids while focusing on one central object or space. By doing so, we would be better equipped to meditate during daily activities without having to close our eyes. I learned that we meditate to train the mind to let deliberate thought come and go. We do not try to prevent thoughts from arising. Letting the thoughts come and go was compared to cars on the freeway. We don't set up a roadblock, nor do we hitch a ride down the freeway. We just notice when we are deliberately thinking about a thought that has arisen and bring our minds back to the "stillness of the heart." When we notice that we are deliberately pushing thoughts away or attempting to force our minds to be quiet, we were to acknowledge that, then relax and let the thoughts come and go. The more we returned to silence, the more we would see that thoughts eventually dissolve. The thoughts may come back and we cannot stop the brain. But regular meditation changes our relationship to the active mind.

It was all so foreign to me. I had never been so stressed about trying to relax. I was used to Catholic Mass, where everything followed the program. Nothing ever changed—the prayers, the songs, the repetition, the communion, the responses, the order. Here, we were left with our own thoughts. It was the opposite of order; it was a spiritual free-for-all. I couldn't hide behind the "Hail Marys" or the "Our Fathers" to avoid facing my feelings.

After 15 minutes, I could feel the radiation moving from my toes to my feet and up my legs. My limbs were falling asleep. I tried clearing my mind, but all I could focus on was the tingling sensation. No one else was moving, and I wondered if they were feeling the same thing I was. I tried to push the discomfort aside with my mind. I tried to soften my eyes, to the point that they nearly softened shut. The man next to me let out a snort before he went into full-on snoring. The woman seated on my other side wasn't faring well either. I could hear the rumbling from her stomach grow progressively louder, practically echoing through the cavernous room.

Again, I was left wondering how Robby was ever able to accomplish this—not just the meditative state, but the sitting part alone. It seemed like days had gone by before one of the monks rang the gong to start the walking meditation. I untwisted my legs and waited for the blood to recirculate, igniting painful prickling throughout my lower body. The walking meditation involved walking even slower than slow motion in a single-file line around the two rows of short wooden dividers that were set up in the temple. For 10 minutes we consciously slowed our movements, as if we were walking while submerged in quicksand, until the gong was heard and we returned to our seated meditation pose for the remaining 20 minutes. When it was over, it took a while for me to amble to the other side of the room. I turned and bowed as people were already lined up to put their cushions away.

Afterward, we all returned to the hall where monks were setting up for a morning service. Two large wooden doors opened as all the resident monks ceremoniously walked out in two lines, taking their seats to begin their regular morning ritual of chanting, lighting incense and bowing. It wasn't bowing for the faint of heart or knees. This was hard-core bowing.

We started from the standing position to a kneeling position, then stretched out our arms over our head, palms and forehead to the floor. It was almost like a downward-dog pose, but with our legs together. We then stood up and repeated the bow several times. We did this throughout the entire 30-minute ceremony. There was also singing, reminiscent of a Catholic Mass. This was unique to this particular practice, as many Buddhist ceremonies do not involve singing. They used western-style chants that are set to a four-part harmony, whereas most Buddhists use a form of chanting that is native to the East.

That first morning, I was more fascinated by the process than anything else. All I knew was that I was far away from Vallejo and far away from Catholicism. And for now, that was enough.

Chapter 13

Be Still

Reverend Master Jisho was sitting near the entrance close to an old-fashioned freestanding fireplace that looked like an enclosed cauldron. A small group of people gathered around it, rubbing their frozen palms together and placing them as close to the heat as possible. Spanning the right wall was a panoramic view of Mount Shasta and its stretch of the Cascade Ridge. Coffee and tea were set up to the side and chairs were placed in rows facing Master Jisho.

I looked at my copy of the agenda: *7:45 a.m.: Questions and Answers. Coffee and tea are offered.*

Master Jisho was a tall, slender man with large glasses and an easygoing demeanor. He had been living at the monastery for several decades now and was one of the senior teachers. I had a lot of questions, but I wasn't ready, and I didn't know where to start.

A soft-spoken woman raised her hand and shared her frustrations with meditation. "I find my mind wandering and I don't know how to center my thoughts."

Master Jisho responded that this is normal, and instead of pushing them away, we should acknowledge our thoughts before releasing them. It was a forgiving response.

"And what about your legs falling asleep?" asked another man.

Yes! I wanted to yell. *What about that?*

He responded that we didn't have to sit cross-legged on the floor, we could sit on chairs, or we could take a booster cushion, which would slightly elevate our legs. There were sounds of relief and muffled laughter throughout the room.

"And what do we do when we can't take the thoughts that are in our heads? What if we want to escape them because they're too painful to sit with?"

I followed the shaky voice and saw a woman in her early 50s with long, chestnut-brown hair. Her voice was cracking with emotion and she paused to compose herself.

"Meditation," Master Jisho responded, "allows us to tap into our 'Buddha nature,' the source of compassion, love and wisdom."

There are thoughts, he explained, whether trivial or deeply painful, that naturally surface in the process. Because we are not accustomed to being still, we are not accustomed to facing these emotions, which are often left buried and unacknowledged. The answer was to keep meditating, and to go against our natural instinct to run. Instead, we should embrace the thoughts and take notice of the emotions they bring up and any physical reactions we may have.

"We have to find a way to be kind to ourselves," he said. "Sit with the pain and approach it with loving compassion." Not doing so, he said, would keep us in the pattern of suffering.

"Nobody wants to suffer. Nobody *should* suffer. Suffering is wanting things to be other than they are. By keeping silent and by meditating, we give ourselves a chance to quiet down, be still and see what's there inside of us so we can acknowledge this suffering and let it go."

I felt a sudden mix of emotions—relief and gratitude and sadness. I took out the brown handkerchief I kept in my pocket and placed it over my eyes. Finally I didn't feel like we were being punished or tested by God—that our suffering wasn't a preordained sentence that we were destined to serve. The pain of losing Robby was there, and would always be there, but the suffering that came with it, my guilt, shame, anger, pity, regret—although natural—was something I could acknowledge and release, eventually. Rather than accept my suffering as God's will, I was allowed to show myself compassion.

A weight was beginning to lift, but I knew it would require what I wasn't yet prepared to offer: forgiveness.

I had to forgive myself for what I believed to be my failures as a mother. And I had to forgive those who took Robby's life. *Forgive those who trespass against us.*

⌒

8:45 a.m.: Full Morning Breakfast.

Reverend Master Shiko sat at the front of the room where three long wooden tables were arranged in a "U" shape. Place settings were already arranged on the tables: a plate, a bowl on top of the plate, and a cup inside the bowl. It reminded me of a Russian matryoshka doll. Silverware was placed crosswise toward the front of the plate.

Master Shiko intrigued me. I didn't expect female monks, and honestly, I didn't expect white monks. I expected men—Asian men—draped in saffron-colored robes. I saw pictures of these monks who had visited the abbey, but during this retreat they were nowhere to be found. In fact, Shasta Abbey was started by an Englishwoman who studied in Malaysia and Japan. The monks here had all grown up in the West, most from America, others from England, Canada, New Zealand and other western places. It was a bit like going to a soul food restaurant and seeing a staff full of Greek people. How authentic could it be? But then I thought of

Robby sitting in the yoga studio and even the women in his class. Yoga was a practice that originated in ancient India more than 5,000 years ago. Not one of them looked like an authentic Indian male yogi.

I got over the visual distraction and focused on the teachings instead, which were aligned with what I had read in Robby's books. But Reverend Master Shiko added another layer of distraction. She had a shaved head like all the other monks and was wrapped in the same beige robe. But unlike the other female monks, her natural coloring made her appear as if she had a light layer of lipstick and a hint of eye makeup. It made me wonder about her life before monkhood—or perhaps a life wished for beyond monkhood. I wondered what brought her here, what caused her to enter the monastic life. Was it a tragedy like mine? Was this all just an escape from the fucked-upness of reality? She sat stone-faced, waiting for everyone to find seats and settle in.

I was looking forward to a break from the emotional discussion earlier, but meals at the monastery were not exempt from Buddhist teachings. It was an intricate, time-consuming process that required one to truly tap into their Zen practice, especially if they were hungry. The process went as follows: First, we were to focus on the lifecycle of the food—where it came from, the hands that planted the seeds, the hands that harvested the fruits and vegetables, the hands that washed the vegetables, the hands that prepared the ingredients and the hands that cooked the meal. The water used to cleanse the food. The people who donated the food to the monastery, and those who donated money that allowed the monks to buy the food. The people it took to package, stock and transport the food. Every process and every person involved in the process.

We were to "think deeply" about all aspects of the food we were about to eat. It was enlightening, if not overwhelming, to fully recognize and appreciate it all. We were welcome to partake in second helpings, though we were asked to be mindful about waste. Only take as much as you can eat, so nothing—not one drop, one bean, one grain, one *anything*—is thrown away.

For each meal, participants sat on both sides of the two long, narrow tables attached to the head table at the front of the room, with a monk at the head of one of the tables. Today, it was Reverend Master Shiko. Booklets were distributed as she loudly clapped two pieces of wood together to mark the beginning of opening "remarks." I call them remarks and not prayers because there was no deity to pray to. Buddha was not a god, he was merely a man who was able to achieve enlightenment, and in that sense, we could all be buddhas who have yet to reach a higher spiritual plane.

Every meal began with everyone reciting the "Five Thoughts":

1. "We must think deeply of the ways and means by which this food has come." *Described above.*

2. "We must consider our merit when accepting it." *What deeds have we done to make us worthy of the work and sacrifice that went into producing the food?*

3. "We must protect ourselves from error by excluding greed from our minds." *Rather than stuff our mouths, we were to take our time and be mindful about the food.*

4. "We will eat lest we become lean and die." *Food has a purpose, to give us nutrition to live.*

5. "We accept this food so that we may become enlightened." *Food is meant to fuel our life; life is meant to pursue enlightenment. Recognizing this relationship brings us closer to that goal.*

Even the unbundling of our place settings was a ritual. During the recital of the Five Thoughts, we slowly lifted the cup and silverware and placed them next to the plate, with as much sound-reducing movement as possible. Volunteers from the kitchen wheeled in two silver carts stocked with all the food, drinks and condiments. One cart was placed at the head of each table. From there, each dish, each drink, each condiment would pass from one person to the other, one by one. Every time you were passed something, you would *gassho* and bow before taking the offering from their hands. After you'd taken some of the food, you would then turn to the person next to you and repeat the process before handing it to them. By the time everything was passed down, you would have bowed your head and *gassho*'d approximately 10 to 12 times. And you were not to begin eating until every item had passed through everyone's hands and found its way back to the silver cart, which was now placed at the end of each table. Second helpings started the process all over again.

At the end of the meal, a moist dishcloth made its way down in the same ritualistic fashion as each of us wiped the crumbs and other traces of food from our space on the table. This was to signify that we are all responsible for our actions. We are accountable, so to speak, for the messes we make, yet we are all interconnected in life. One uncleansed spot could affect the whole appearance of the table.

After the meal and cleaning were complete, we were asked to stay and wait for our names to be called for our individual assignments. There was no fee to participate in the retreat, but we were expected to help in the daily operations of the abbey while we were there. I was assigned to the kitchen, cleaning and chopping vegetables. Wiping down the counters and mopping floors. Every action, no matter how seemingly menial, required mindfulness. Water used to wash the vegetables would have to be dumped into large buckets where the monks would later use it to water plants. Any scrap of food waste, down to an ounce of cilantro stems, would have to be carried over for composting. Absolutely nothing went to waste.

"Oh, no!" the woman in front of me yelled out.

I jumped back and gasped. We had been working in silence now for more than an hour. A mere whisper would have startled me.

She lifted her cupped hands from the large metal bowl where she had been separating Italian parsley leaves from their stems. Water was now dripping through her fingers and onto the newly mopped floor. "Oh, no!" she yelled again.

"What's wrong?" asked one of the other workers.

She opened her palms to reveal a small insect now writhing in a drop of water.

"Just bring it outside," whispered the other woman once she squinted and realized what all the fuss was about.

One of the earlier dharma talks was focused on karma, and how every living thing on Earth deserved to be treated with respect and compassion. Even the tiniest of creatures, say, in a bundle of herbs, could be a human experiencing rebirth. And because they may not have lived the most compassionate life, they were now starting at the bottom and working their way back up the chain. If you killed them, then you would now have bad karma. I thought this was the concept of reincarnation, but I was wrong. This, I was told, was a Hindu idea. Instead, Buddhism used the concept of "rebirth," which is slightly different. In reincarnation a self goes from life to life. The Buddha taught that the concept of a "self" is an illusion. There is "habit energy" that passes from life to life, but not a self. It was a mind-bender for me—a riddle I had yet to solve.

I didn't quite know what to make of it. I was dealing with my son's death, and she was yelling over an insect in the parsley bowl. I had a lot of work to do, apparently.

Cicero was assigned outdoors in the snow, where he would take bundles of split wood stacked along the cloister and carry them over to an area covered by a large tarp. This would protect the wood from moisture and help ensure a steady source of heat for the monks during the long winter at the abbey.

We went through our "working meditation" for an hour and a half before our next meditation at Buddha Hall. I stopped by a clipboard with a sign-up sheet for people who wanted to request private spiritual counseling and wrote my name on it.

I entered Buddha Hall, this time grabbing a booster cushion, sat in meditation pose facing the wall and allowed myself to sit with my pain. I acknowledged it, the grief, the longing, the anger, the helplessness. I wept, forcing myself to focus on an area of the cream-colored wall in front of me. I heard Robby's voice: *Free your mind.*

All the despair came flooding in, as if my sitting still allowed it to rise and rage over the dam, mercilessly taking my body along with it, and leaving it to thrash violently in its force. I felt the physical pain in my chest, my back, my head, my neck, my shoulders. I was drowning. I wanted to yell out. I wanted to die. But I remained still, allowing it to wash over me until the sound of the singing bowl rang through the hall, traveling from my ears and into my gathered palms, like a lifeline waiting for me to grab hold.

Chapter 14

Baby Buddha

Reverend Master Kodo and I were engaged in a staring contest. It was nearing the end of Day Two of the retreat, and I was sitting in the common room of the guest area, drinking a cup of lemon tea in silence.

"You signed up for private spiritual counseling?" she whispered.

I raised my eyes, mid-sip. "Oh," was all I could muster.

Now that the moment had come, I really didn't know what to say. I was tempted to tell her I had changed my mind. *Nothing to see here; keep walking.*

But she already was walking, across the room and out the door. I placed my cup of tea on the square table in front of me and hurried to catch up. I followed her along the path and into her office. It was a cozy space with soft yellow lighting and floor-to-ceiling shelves packed with rows of books that seemed to span generations of wisdom. I took a seat facing her.

"What would you like to discuss?" she asked. This is when the staring contest officially began.

I examined her face, sweet and gentle. She wore silver-rimmed glasses and had a slight gap between her two front teeth. I imagined her with a head full of hair, playing with her young grandchildren or lunching somewhere with her longtime girlfriends. But she was here, sans hair, by choice, and she sat patiently as I tried to find the words. I wasn't used to people being okay with long periods of silence. I expected her to prod me more. I wanted her to break the silence. But I was dealing with a monk. We could've stayed this way for hours without a word spoken between us.

"My son," I began. I could already feel my throat tightening. I waited awhile before trying again as her serene gaze remained unbroken. "My son was shot and killed just two months ago. And I just don't understand. I don't understand how something like this can happen to him, to our family." By now I was sobbing uncontrollably.

Master Kodo placed her palms together to her heart. She looked genuinely pained.

"Oh, my dear," she said, now pressing her right palm flatly against her chest. She sat back and waited for me to continue.

"I don't know why I'm here, but I think Robby wants me to be here. I've been reading his books and he was practicing Buddhism and meditation. I want to understand him. I want to feel like I'm continuing his journey. But I just don't know what the point is anymore."

I waited for her to speak, but she only looked at me, making sure I had said everything I wanted to say.

"I'm trying," I continued. "I'm trying to follow his footsteps, but sometimes it's just too painful. I'm angry that this happened and I'm afraid because I don't know who did this. I feel spiritually lost. I don't have faith anymore."

My sobs were unrelenting, and I was convinced they reverberated throughout the abbey, pounding on doors and bursting into Buddha Hall, shattering the fragile bubble of serenity the monastery offered.

"My dear," she started, placing her hand on mine. "There are no answers to why these things happen. You are here, and that shows you have a stronger faith than you are able to realize. By coming here you are continuing his path and honoring him. Your son led you here. The path you are following is his last gift to you." She opened the top drawer of her desk and brought out a Buddhist prayer bracelet made of wood. It didn't matter, she said, if I was Catholic praying the rosary or Buddhist or Muslim, the prayer beads would help calm me, even if I just went through each bead and counted my breathing.

It was a prayer bracelet similar to one I had seen in Robby's room, alongside his rosary beads. She placed the bracelet in my palm, holding my hand between both her palms. "You cannot change what has happened. It is how you deal with the pain that will ultimately free you from suffering."

I left Master Kodo's office, seeing sadness in her eyes. Seeing a disappointment in humanity that perhaps led her to this life. I veered off the trail toward the snow and kept walking until I found myself under a canopy of towering pine trees, providing a natural shield and sound barrier between me and the abbey. I sat in meditative pose preparing to sit in silence, but instead yelled as loudly as I could until my voice went hoarse. And even then I continued to yell.

⌐

A festival ceremony marked the last day of the retreat, where all the monks and participants gathered at Buddha Hall reviewing the highlights of our sessions and sharing our final thoughts. Now that we had graduated from the Introductory Retreat, the monks welcomed us to return to the abbey to participate in any future retreats or ceremonies. The abbey was also available for extended stays for those who wished to deepen their practice at the monastery. Lay residents would be allowed to join in the daily activities of meditation, working meditation, ceremonies and dharma talks.

It was tempting.

I didn't know when or if there would be a trial in Robby's case. As far as I knew there were no arrests or leads yet. But if it ever came to that, I pictured myself showing up at the abbey, prepared to work in the kitchen, sit in silence, wake up in the pre-dawn hours to the sound of a singing bowl. I would stay there until the trial was over and I wouldn't have to hear or deal with anything about the case again. But I didn't know what would be more difficult. Being out there dealing with the outside noise. Or being in here, left to piece together the wreckage of my psyche.

I suppose what the retreat taught me was that, no matter the external circumstance, I would need to find a way to keep my mental, intellectual and spiritual house in order. Whether that meant sitting in a courtroom hearing about my son's death or sitting in a dark meditation room facing the tempest of my emotions. Both required a level of fortitude that I wasn't sure I had.

Being still was the first step. This was the foundation I would need to deal with myself and everything around me.

The next was understanding that I had a clear decision to make: wake up each morning fueled by hate and revenge, or wake up fueled by love and forgiveness. It wasn't as easy as good over evil, right over wrong. How do you forgive someone who took your child? How do you forgive someone you don't even know?

It would have been much easier to choose hate. Much easier to wish suffering upon those responsible for our pain. But I was committed to taking the other path because I knew the rest of Julie's life depended on it. She already lost her brother. I could not rob her of her mother.

The ceremony was a departure in tone from the retreat. There were gongs and bells and incense and bowing, and a general feeling of celebration and ceremony. We were given handfuls of colorful confetti to throw as we followed the monks in a figure-eight pattern throughout the hall with the beat of a large *taiko*, a Japanese drum. The confetti represented lotus petals and were made of silver- and gold-colored construction paper. For the monastery, this was practically a full-on club scene.

While people lined up to place their incense at the altar, one of the senior monks, Reverend Master Jisho, walked over to me and asked me to follow him.

"Are you Pati?" he asked. I nodded. "Can you come with me, please?"

I looked over at Cicero, who looked just as confused as I was. I followed Reverend Master Jisho through the hall where there was a narrow door tucked behind a corner toward the back. I hadn't noticed it before, but most of the time we spent in the hall was in darkness. The long, narrow room had a simple maple desk and two chairs.

"Reverend Master Kodo says that you lost your son?"

I nodded.

"We discussed this after our morning meditation with the monastic community here, and we would like to offer your son a Buddhist ceremony since he was practicing Buddhism. I know you had a funeral for him already. You can invite your family and we can have it here in Buddha Hall."

I was deeply moved, and I knew it was something Robby would have wanted. I told him I would speak to the rest of my family so we could agree on a date, thanking him for his kindness and feeling greatly humbled by it.

"You know, my sister lost her son not too long ago—my nephew," he said. "He was around your son's age. She was distraught, of course, but you know what she said to me? She said, 'He was never really mine.'"

The story resonated with me, because even though I gave birth to him, I never believed he was mine. He belonged to the universe, to humanity. He was a part of me, but he was not mine.

"Why do you think such bad things happen to good people?" I asked.

"It's just karma," he responded. "Someone out there shoots someone else and someone else has to pay the price of that bad karma. Maybe he was paying the price for someone else's karma."

I didn't accept that answer. It was then that I vowed not to ever seek an answer to that question again. Every religion will have its own answer, and none of them will be acceptable. Instead, I would focus on how these different practices could help me deal with the rest of my life and how I would learn and grow from this tragedy. There was one story, however, that Reverend Master Jisho shared with me that touched me deeply.

In the Buddha's lifetime, he said, a relative of his lost her newborn baby. She was consumed with grief and asked him to bring her baby back to life. He said he would, if she could find a house in the city where they never had a family member die. When she realized that everyone knows death, she felt she was not alone and brought her baby back to the Buddha for a ceremony and burial.

Less than two weeks later, we returned to Shasta Abbey with a group of about 15 family members to attend Robby's Buddhist memorial ceremony. We all met at Ruben's house and left at 7:00 a.m., hoping to arrive early for the noon ceremony. We took four cars, stopping only for gas and bathroom breaks. I was shocked that everyone came, particularly my mom, who was a devout Catholic.

The monks placed Robby's picture at the foot of a large painting of Guanyin, the bodhisattva associated with compassion. Each monk approached the altar, placing incense before Robby's picture before inviting each of us to come up and do the same. It was a memorial ceremony offered specifically for people who died a tragic death to help ease their journey up the spiritual ladder. This was very similar to the intention of the Nine Days. Ruben, Cicero and I thanked each of the monks as we shared cakes and tea afterward. Julie sat next to Reverend Master Kodo, showing her the prayer beads that she now wore around her wrist. I thanked Master Reverend Jisho for leading the ceremony and allowing us to bring our family.

"Now Robby is a baby Buddha," he said. "I am sure he is smiling."

I warmed at the thought. Robby's interest in Buddhism led us all here to this place. And though I could no longer see him, I knew wherever he was, he was smiling.

I imagined this was faith.

～

PSYCHOTHERAPY NOTE
  *CHIEF COMPLAINT:
  Pati D Poblete is a 44 Y female who returned to focus on addressing symptoms involving: PTSD, grief
  *Updated Clinical Status/Relevant History/Active Abuse-Trauma Concerns/Treatment Response: Pati reports she is reading many of son's books and exploring outside of her own religion and seeking answers. She has repeated flashbacks of son's shooting.
  Status of target symptoms: According to Pati, since the last visit these symptoms have been improved.

Life

Chapter 15

I'm Still Here

The duffel bags were already piled up by the door, waiting to make their way back to Ruben's house before returning here in a week. It was the new normal after the divorce: one week at my house, one week at his, and so on for who knew how long.

I felt guilty every Sunday, watching Robby and Julie collect their things, stuffing them into their bags, scanning their rooms for anything else they might need for the week. It was an arrangement Ruben and I came up with together, to leave things simple and out of the courts. Easy for us but not so much for them. I saw the guilt in their eyes, too, having to leave one parent for the other. It was a routine they would continue up until Robby began working with his dad. By then it just made sense for them to commute together, so Robby stayed with Ruben during the week, stopping by my house here and there to visit me, spend the weekend or just drop in for a meal.

Robby was always more vocal than Julie in expressing his struggles with transitioning between houses over the years.

"If it's that hard for you, you can just stay with your dad. I promise, I won't be hurt. I know it's hard," I assured him. It was the summer before his first year of high school.

"It's not that easy," he said, tearing up. "You can't expect us to just pick one parent and live with them, even if you say it's okay. It makes us feel bad."

He was right. It wasn't fair. I tried to explain that this was the only way we could avoid going to court. If it was easier, I said, they could spend longer times between houses, maybe two weeks, maybe a month before switching to the other house.

"You don't understand," he said. "I feel like I don't belong any-where, like I don't have a home."

It pained my heart to hear those words. And yet, I still could not come up with an answer. Would it have been better if we had never divorced? But how healthy would that have been? I second-guessed everything. I held myself responsible.

"You don't think Julie feels the same way?" he asked. "It's hard for her, too. She just doesn't say anything."

For a decade they straddled the two worlds, each home pos-sessing half of their belongings, half of their set of parents, as they lugged their necessities in between. It was during this time that Robby and Julie understood that no matter what, they were the only constants in each other's lives. The surroundings would change, the parent would change depending on the week, but one thing never changed: They were together. Their shared circum-stance bonded them, and yet they could not be more different from each other.

Ever since their personalities took shape, I knew they were opposites. Robby was shy and introspective. Julie was social and outgoing. Robby ate only the yolk of his over-easy eggs, while Julie only ate the white portion. He ate the broccoli tops, while she only ate the stems. Julie played team sports in high school and made many friends. Robby kept only a few close friends, saying that he wasn't interested in quantity over quality. Julie enjoyed popular music. Robby was into anything but mainstream—his playlists included everything from classical to jazz, from old-school blues to alternative rock.

I once handed each of them a blank piece of white construction paper and a watercolor paint set. "I want both of you to paint a picture for me so I can hang them by my desk at work," I instructed. Julie was nine, Robby 11. They took their sheets and paint sets and headed into their rooms. After an hour I checked back with them. Robby handed me his paper, which was transformed into a winter moonscape from space. He painted the background all black, with silver stars and a glowing yellow moon illuminating the dark space over a snow-covered planet Earth. Julie handed me her sheet, a bright, summer day, complete with a blue sky, birds in flight, a bright sun and a flowing stream lined with colorful flowers. Literally night and day, summer and winter. They were different in every way imaginable. Yet one could not exist without the other.

"You always said I was brave," Julie said during her eulogy. "But I guess I was brave because I always knew you would catch me if I fell."

After Robby's death, Julie was a blur, helping with funeral arrangements, surrounding herself with friends and family. I knew it was what she needed to do to stay afloat. Several weeks after the funeral, she found me in Robby's room sitting on the floor. She took a seat next to me and placed her head on my shoulder, as she did many times when she was just a young girl. "There were things that only Robby and I shared," she said, crying. "We were like yin and yang. Now it's just me. How can there be a yin without a yang?"

⌒

IKEA was packed with people stopping from one design showroom to the next, pushing wide carts filled with random items, discussing measurements, shelves and closet spaces. We made a curious foursome, Julie, Ruben, Cicero and me. My past and my future converging to create an unconventional present. We got along fine before, but after Robby's death we all seemed to pull ourselves up onto the same lifeboat, and we clung to one another now for survival.

A month after the funeral, Julie decided she would resume her second year of school at the Fashion Institute of Design & Merchandising (FIDM) in San Francisco, even though Ruben, Cicero and I were on extended leaves from work. I was still on psychological disability, while Ruben had amassed countless hours of paid time off over the years. Cicero was in the red, using time off that he had yet to earn. But Julie was adamant. She would finish school for her brother.

She found an apartment in Alameda, about a 20-minute commute to school, as opposed to the 90-plus minutes it would have taken her to commute during rush-hour traffic from our home. We were all reluctant to let her go. This was still a very fragile time, and I think we needed her more than we thought she needed us.

I was worried about her being on her own, especially now. Her panic attacks were more severe and more frequent than mine. But a solution presented itself when my cousin, Andrew Baigan, found a job at a nearby hospital and offered to be her roommate. It worked out for both of them, and having them together helped ease our worries. At just 21 years old, Julie was fighting to keep her head above water by resuming life and moving to a place where no one knew her, no one knew about what happened. She could start fresh.

"What about this one?" she called out, standing by the "Malm" model—a low, full-size bed with built-in nightstands and magazine slots on each side. We all walked over, nodding our heads in approval, trying our best to make the trip as "normal" as possible.

"That looks good," I said.

"Whatever you want," added Ruben.

We wrote down the make and model on a sheet of paper before searching for the boxed parts on the ground floor. Along the way we picked up items for her new kitchen, bathroom and living room. We offered spare furniture from our houses—a patio set for her balcony from Ruben's house. A coffee table, kitchen appliances and a rug from our house.

We made the drive over to her new apartment, unloading the boxes while Ruben put together her new bed. Under different circumstances, this would have been a more joyous occasion, filled with picture-taking and lighthearted advice about laundry and always keeping a toilet plunger handy. We were all relieved that she was still motivated to go to school, even though we assured her that she could take as much time off as she needed.

"No," she responded. "I want to finish."

"Then you're stronger than all of us," Ruben told her.

On weekends, and sometimes weeknights, Cicero, Ruben and I would make the 45-minute drive together to her apartment to have dinner with her, go out for ice cream or offer an all-expense-paid trip to Target.

"I'm just going to change real quick," she yelled out from her room one night when I came on my own to spend time with her.

I rose from her futon to the kitchen to get a glass of water. On the counter was a flickering candle where she had set up an altar for her brother with his picture. He was wearing his favorite black and green University of Hawaii football jersey, flashing a big smile. In her room I noticed books on mindfulness, Buddhism and meditation. She had prayer flags hanging on her wall with the seven chakras, similar to the flags Robby had hung in his own room. I realized we were all following his footsteps.

We spent as much time with her as we could, making sure she knew we were there for her, while protecting her from anything that may upset her: updates from the detectives, stories about our own grief and inability to return to life. We coddled and alienated her at the same time, though we didn't realize it. But she knew. She knew there were things we weren't telling her and emotions we weren't showing her. She felt responsible for us all, her three parents, shouldering the burden that she thought she would share with her brother one day, far into the future when we were no longer able to care for ourselves. But that day was now, and it was too much to bear the burden alone while tending to her own wounds. So she moved away, and though it was difficult to let her go, I knew it was something she had to do.

Nobody wanted to go through the holidays. What was there to be thankful for on Thanksgiving? The thought of Christmas was excruciating. New Year's Eve—the worst year of our lives was coming to an end, and we were entering 2015 with shattered hopes and broken spirits. I would have preferred to drink myself to sleep at 8:00 p.m. But Ruben, Cicero and I decided collectively that we would at least go through Thanksgiving and Christmas. And we would spend them together, all the families for each holiday.

Since Ruben and I divorced, Robby and Julie would have to split time between families during the holidays. I knew it was hard for them, and it always pained me. This year, we would all be together, for Robby and for Julie. But it didn't ease the pain. I thought of Robby every Christmas counting the number of presents under the tree marked for him, then counting Julie's to make sure they were exactly even. If Julie had just one more present, he would make it known.

"I see Julie has eight presents and I have seven," he said when he was just nine years old. And every year since I'd catch him under the tree taking inventory.

I didn't know if I should hang his stocking, which I'd fill with candy and random stocking stuffers every year. It didn't feel right to not hang it.

There was no joy in this holiday. Everything Christmas represented—peace, faith, hope—was elusive to us in the rawness of our loss.

"I'm still here," Julie said, as we all sat around, just waiting for the holiday to end.

It was a statement she made several times afterward, and I realized that despite all our efforts, she felt left behind by her brother and abandoned by us as we grieved for him. After the holidays were over, I decided to plan something for just the four of us.

~

January 1, 2015, was a clear and crisp day. The sun hung high above Lake Merritt, a tidal lagoon surrounded by parkland in the heart of Oakland. We pedaled along a path that outlined the lake's 3.4-mile heart-shaped shoreline, taking in the shimmering reflections that bounced off the water like bobbing diamonds strewn across the surface. Robby loved cycling, and I thought a bike ride around the lake on New Year's Day would be the perfect way to honor him. Julie was riding her new bike that Ruben just bought her for Christmas, Cicero and I were riding bikes that Robby helped pick, and Ruben was riding his bike, which had sparked Robby's interest in cycling in the first place. We circled the lake twice, stopping by a gazebo where Ruben attempted some old bike tricks.

"Man, I'm getting old," he said after almost falling twice.

After our second lap around the lake, we stopped for lunch at Lake Chalet, a renovated boathouse that was now a waterfront restaurant with a long wooden pier that stretched over the water. We sat at our table with the sound of seagulls and the smell of seafood surrounding us, exhausted and exhilarated by the bike ride. We sipped our iced teas and ate off one another's plates, listening to Julie's stories about her teachers and fellow students. She went through her different impersonations of them, a skill she claimed was "God-given," and we laughed.

We laughed openly and unabashedly, finding happiness and comfort in the fact that, despite everything, she was still here. And because of her, so were we.

Chapter 16

Passport

I was among the first real guests at the Vivanta by Taj Hotel in Gurgaon, about 20 miles from New Delhi. Just a week prior, there was a soft launch attended by friends and family of staff and the owners. But today, February 12, 2013, was the real deal, and the staff were practically falling over each other to make sure each guest was properly cared for. For every person checking in, there were about five waitstaff close by, offering water, candy, a napkin to wipe the bead of sweat from your brow. "Anything at all, ma'am, I am most happy to be of your service," said one of the workers, nodding his head sideways from shoulder to shoulder, a habit I had unconsciously adopted by the end of my trip. Surrounded by aging buildings and crumbling infrastructure, the opulent structure looked like a sparkling diamond that had finally formed after years of industrial pressure. Known as the "Millennium City," the Gurgaon district was emerging as the economic capital of India—the luxury five-star hotel was evidence of that. I entered the lavish hotel lobby dazed, confused and ready to collapse. The total travel time from San Francisco International Airport was more than 23 hours, and I had barely slept the whole trip. I spent most of my time on the plane preparing my presentations for the three-day conference, where I was invited to speak on environmental challenges in Southeast Asia and potential areas of work on sustainability issues in India.

"Welcome to our hotel, ma'am," said the impeccably dressed man behind the front desk. "We are most happy to welcome you as one of our first guests." I smiled in return, pushing my passport across the polished marble counter. I didn't feel worthy of being one of their first guests. My hair was disheveled, my skin was greasy and verging on a major acne breakout, my clothes were wrinkled. I did not scream "five-star guest."

Nevertheless, four porters were called to bring my two pieces of luggage to my room. We rode up the elevator together, squeezed in the square space lined with lacquered wood and mirrors capturing every awkward smile. "So," I offered, "you just opened?" "Yes!" they all answered at once, looking genuinely happy. When the elevator finally opened, they motioned for me to go first while each of them held one end of each bag. I watched two of the porters carrying my small duffel bag, inside of which were my hair straightener, a couple of pairs of shoes and an assortment of bras and underwear. "I can take that," I offered. "No, ma'am. Please, no," one of them responded.

When we reached my room, one of the men swiped the key card and motioned for me to enter. It was the most lavish hotel room I had ever stayed in, accented with mahogany panels, glass and stone. The room was filled with rich colors of topaz, burgundy and saffron, with a huge window that spanned the length of one wall. I turned to see the four men patiently waiting. "Oh!" I said, scrambling to find my wallet. I gave them each a tip as they placed their palms together, bowed and turned to leave. I turned toward the window, looking out across the city. Directly across the street was the railway originating from the nearby Huda City Centre Metro

Station. I watched a long train go by, cutting through the haze of smog that hovered over the city and stretched across the horizon. Sandwiched between areas of blight were new structures, cranes and scaffolding, all pointing to a city in transition.

I took out my iPhone, took pictures of the view and the room and sent them with a message: "Robby, Julie: I'm here."

"Yay! Have fun. Love you," Julie responded.

"Cool. Have a good trip. I hope I can come on the next trip there. Love you," Robby responded.

The next morning, I cracked open the heavy door of my room, hooking my arm around and reaching for the canvas bag that held the morning newspaper. I had become an expert at sliding these bags off the doorknob without being seen in the hallway in my bathrobe. I shuffled back to the large desk in my room, rolled the rubber band from my February 13, 2013, copy of The Times of India and scanned the headlines with my jet-lagged eyes.

2 Held in Wazirganj Double Murder Case

Railways plan additional temporary station for Kumbh

Nashik Municipal Corporation to undertake road works before monsoon

None of those stories would work. In just five hours I would be giving a presentation to a number of representatives from India's national government on the need to monitor and manage their natural resources, as they did the country's economy. But I needed a hook. I needed something that was actually happening in their country to make it real.

And then I saw it: chickens. There, squeezed between ads on an inside page was a brief article on the rise of chicken prices in Hubli, the second largest city in the southwest state of Karnataka. Local poultry farmers attributed the hike in prices to several trends, namely the bird flu attack in Bangalore and the increase in prices in bird feed. I could work with that. Bird feed was based on different grains, which were grown on agricultural land. But due to rapid development throughout the country, agricultural lands were dwindling to make room for housing, commercial buildings, roads and other infrastructure. This meant the country was becoming more dependent on imported grain. Hence, the rise in prices in bird feed and at chicken stalls throughout the region. So how could the country continue to grow economically while still meeting its population's demand on poultry? The easy answer would be to increase their imports, but it was still a low-income country that would be vulnerable to volatile food prices at the global level. Yes! I put the paper down with a sense of relief and confidence. I found an opener.

Because of my journalism background I wanted to pull in current events when I spoke so that it was relevant to the audience. And so I could speak to something concrete and not conceptual. Over the years I gained more confidence and finding a point of entry with each audience became easier and easier.

It was this need to find relevance and a connection to people that led to my unlikely leap from a communications director to the head of our Asia outreach and project development. During Global Footprint Network's international conference in Siena, Italy, in June 2010, I was tasked with creating all the collateral materials for the conference, reaching out to speakers and writing articles on the varying panel discussions to put on our website. On the last day of the conference, I spotted three men sitting at a table outside the conference rooms. One man remained standing, holding a booklet, while the other two men sat in chairs, hands folded and placed on the table before them. They were all dressed in what looked like traditional clothes from some part of Southeast Asia.

"Can I help you?" I asked. "We are waiting to speak with Mathis," they responded, referring to our president. I knew Mathis was preparing to catch his flight and would not have time to speak with them. I took a seat across from them and explained that Mathis was pulled away unexpectedly but that I was available to meet with them. I said I was a director—I just didn't say it was for communications. Immediately, the three men went into ceremony mode, standing up and motioning for the third man, who was already standing, to present me with his booklet as the other man snapped a photo of him handing it to me. The three men were from the Indonesian Ministry of Public Works, where they had undergone their own study of the country's ecological situation. Because I had been writing articles on our work for more than a year now, I understood the issues and suggested that the ministry work directly with Global Footprint Network to verify their findings and create a sustainability strategy moving forward. They agreed, and they specifically requested that the "Asia regional director" be their direct contact. And so my title changed—and from then on, I was charged with all new business in the region.

The first time I was sent to give a presentation was before representatives of various United Nations agencies in Bangkok, including the United Nations Development Programme (UNDP), United Nations Environment Programme (UNEP) and the United Nations Economic and Social Commission for Asia and the Pacific (UNESCAP). Nothing like easing me into the job. France's representative scowled at me. Japan's representative skewered me. "What do you mean Japan has a high footprint? What are you suggesting we do?" I pointed to the time-trend data from our researchers on both the supply and demand of natural resources in Japan. They were clearly in the red, as most developed nations were. But he didn't like it. "Look," I wanted to say, "it's not personal. We turn on our air conditioners, waste tons of water on golf courses, produce an enormous amount of food waste and carbon emissions, too. I use paper towels to dry my hands!" Instead, I willed the moisture on my top lip from forming into a full bead of sweat and responded, "Japan has an opportunity to reverse these trends, and I know that managing resources is a priority for your government. We would like to work with you on that." He begrudgingly sat back, the crease between his brows slowly softening. Later that night, he sat next to me during our dinner cruise down the Chao Phraya River lined by Buddhist temples that glowed like white gold in the night. By the end of the evening, we were exchanging business cards. "Call me if you come to Tokyo," he said. "Maybe we can work together on a project for Japan."

∽

After that debut trip, I was in a different country almost every other month, sometimes giving presentations in three different countries within two weeks' time. "That's cool, Mom," Robby said. He was sitting in front of me, in a one-man show playing my audience. "It's like you're out there changing the world." It was a gross overstatement, but I hesitated to adjust his level of appreciation. I remember watching my father get ready for work every morning, his coiffed hair shaped perfectly with pomade. I'd watch him in his dark suits with his black Samsonite briefcase in one hand. I'd inhale the mixed scent of aftershave and coffee that I had come to associate with him. "C'mon," he'd say. "Time to go to school. I have a meeting." I had no idea what he did, but through my nine-year-old eyes, he was larger than life. He was my hero. And though I didn't deserve the title, I felt that my son now looked at me in that same way. But it meant more because he wasn't nine, he was almost 22.

"This presentation is for India," I told him. His face lit up. "Do you think I can come with you?" The trip was just two weeks away, and he didn't have a passport. "I think it's too late for this trip,"

I told him, "but I know I'll be going back so let's get your passport now so you can come next time." He agreed, though he was visibly disappointed. I made an appointment to have his passport photo taken and to submit his application. "Where are you going?" the woman at the post office asked him as she positioned him for his photo. "I'm going to go with my mom to India," he responded. "India! Wow, lucky you," she responded. By the time I had to leave for my trip, Robby had put together a list of things he wanted me to bring back: Indian prayer mat, a tapestry to hang on his wall and spices, spices, spices.

"Anything else?" I asked after he gave me the list. "No," he responded. "I can see what's there when I come with you next time."

Robby's passport was issued in September 2013. He never got a chance to use it.

Chapter 17

Back to Work

Julie and I were racing to place our shoes and laptops in the gray plastic bins at San Francisco International Airport. In all my years of traveling for work, I had come to dread going through security, with airport workers barking orders and moving herds of people along. Stressed and confused travelers trying to keep up the pace while tracking their belongings.

"You can't bring that in here, sir!" an airport security officer yelled, pointing at a man carrying bottled water. Agitated, he looked around for a trash can while trying to keep his place in the long, winding line.

I had resisted going on another international trip since I returned to work in January. The thought of being stuck in the chaotic crowds at the airport, experiencing sudden turbulence on the plane, and being alone in a hotel room—none of which bothered me before—was enough to trigger a panic attack. And I didn't know if I had enough conjuring power to summon Oprah and Maya overseas.

The two-and-a-half-week trip involved three countries: Thailand, Indonesia and the Philippines. I would be meeting with national government agencies and giving presentations on our work as it applied to their environmental policies. I had done it numerous times before, but this time I was terrified.

Ruben and I both diagnosed ourselves with having extensive brain damage. It seemed we had lost large parts of our memories. I had developed an inexplicable and frustrating habit of stuttering. Neither one of us could focus, repeating ourselves and asking the same questions within minutes. I would zone out and stare into space, mid-conversation, not remembering what was even being discussed. At times, I literally could not find the words. I knew in my head what I wanted to say, but I couldn't think of the words to express myself. But here I was, on my way to meet with government officials.

"Everything will be hard the first time," my boss said. "I read that it's better to just put yourself out there and continue work. Otherwise you will fall into depression."

After I had exhausted all the excuses I could think of for not going—and failed—Cicero, Julie and I came up with a plan. Julie would join me the first week in Thailand. Cicero would fly and meet me the second week in Indonesia, which fell on Robby's birthday on April 1. I would be alone for the final leg of my trip to the Philippines, but I had a colleague and friends in Manila, so I really wouldn't be alone.

"Can we go to the floating markets? And can we see the elephants?" Julie asked.

My trips to Bangkok had always been packed with meetings and presentations. My sightseeing knowledge was limited to the famous Reclining Buddha at Wat Pho, the massive malls and areas accessible via Bangkok's Metropolitan Rapid Transit (MRT) that ran along the main artery of Sukhumvit Road. But this was her break before her last quarter at school, and floating markets and elephants were the least I could offer her.

⌒

My first meeting was with representatives of various government agencies and NGOs, hosted by Thailand's Ministry of Environment. There were 20-plus people, notebooks and pens poised, facing the front of a conference room where a projector and screen were already set up for my presentation. Julie came along to help distribute materials. I wore a black suit that day. A black suit in Bangkok's sweltering tropical heat. I was silently beating myself up as my sweat-drenched blouse melted into my torso. But then Reverend Master Jisho's voice rang through my head: *Be kind to yourself.*

It's not your fault, I assured myself. *You have brain damage.*

I researched the country's situation at least a week before the trip and read my notes repeatedly on the plane. The Thai population had steadily increased its beef consumption over the years. As a result, more agricultural land was needed to grow corn to feed cattle, which in turn meant less cropland to grow food for its residents. This meant they had to rely more on imports, which translated to higher prices. My job was to point to this domino effect and suggest ways they could monitor and manage the impact of their changing land-use decisions on their environment and their economy. I was beyond ready.

The director of the Ministry began his opening remarks in Thai before introducing me in English. And then my mind went completely blank. I had no idea what to say or how to start my presentation. I didn't remember anything I had researched about the country's environmental issues, and I had no idea how to connect their work with ours. I felt a sudden pang of guilt, too. *Why was I here in this country? Why was I traveling at all? I should be home grieving. I should be at the cemetery. How can I be back at work as if nothing happened?*

"Please welcome Pati," he said before the crowd began clapping.
Crap.

I put my hand in my pocket and reached for the wooden prayer
bracelet from the abbey. I began thumbing through the beads one
by one, counting my breaths as I approached the podium. I inhaled
and exhaled deeper, slowing my breathing and my heart rate.

"Thank you for inviting me here today," I started. And then a
switch turned on. I was on autopilot. It was as if my hard drive
rebooted, recovering all my missing files and data.

And it felt good.

It felt good to know I could still function. It felt good to know
that I still had something to contribute. But above all, it felt good
to know that no one in this room, no one in this country knew
what happened. I could act like nothing happened, because to
them, nothing did happen. There was no judgment, no pity, no
personal questions. I could be myself without worrying if my facial
expressions were appropriate or if I made people uncomfortable.
People didn't have to avoid me because they didn't know what to
say. Here, Julie and I could just *be*.

By the end of the week, I had attended several meetings without
incident at the large UN building in the center of the bustling
Rajadamnern Avenue. I met with three men—none of whom were
originally from Thailand—who were working on a global sustainable rice project and exploring ways to work with us to monitor the
impact of global rice consumption on the environment. And then
I met with a woman from France who had been living in Thailand
for three years now to work on the UN's sustainability development goals, which were a universal call to action to end poverty
and protect the planet "and ensure that all people enjoy peace and
prosperity."

I hired a private driver to bring Julie and me to the floating
markets at Damnoen Saduak, a three-hour drive outside Bangkok,

then afterward to see the elephants at the ancient city of Ayutthaya. Along the way, a giant critter that resembled a cricket landed on the hood of the car and remained planted there, facing the driver as the car sped down the freeway.

"Good luck," he said, pointing at it through the windshield. "That good luck!" He looked both amazed and concerned. "I cannot kill it. It cannot die," he said. He began veering toward the side of the freeway and pulled over. He opened his door and approached the good luck charm, slowly and delicately shooing it so it would fly away from the freeway, avoiding an untimely death.

"Very good luck," he said, returning to the car.

Julie and I looked at each other. "Maybe it's Robby," I said, smiling.

"Maybe it is," she said.

We arrived at the floating markets, climbing into a long, narrow wooden boat with a small engine. Our guide for the day was a short, older man with bare, calloused feet. He took us through a series of canals bordered by wooden houses on stilts, hanging laundry and lazy pets sitting on sunlit porches watching the boats go by. Julie sat toward the front of the boat, recording everything with her iPhone.

After about 10 or 15 minutes, the boat turned a corner and it was as if everything came alive. Like that moment in *The Wizard of Oz* when Dorothy went from black and white to vibrant color. The waterway was packed with other boats, some filled with tourists, others with vendors selling hot pad Thai noodles, bowls of spicy soup, fresh-cut mangoes and bananas, young coconuts with straws to extract their sweet, delicate juice. On either side of the waterway were rows and rows of stalls. Paintings, local artifacts, spices, wood carvings. It was a gift-giver's dream.

We learned quickly not to make eye contact unless we were sure we wanted something. One locked gaze would prompt "the hook," as Julie and I called it. If a vendor saw you looking, he or she would pull out a long wooden stick with a metal hook at the end of it, grabbing hold of the side of your boat and reeling you in for a sale.

We soaked in the colors, the smells, the noise, the *life* of it all. Our boat navigated through the intricate labyrinth of waterways, taking us from one aisle of local treasures to the next until we had filled our senses and emptied our wallets. After about three hours, we met the driver at the parking lot where he had been waiting. We brought him food and drinks, and he accepted them shyly, sitting down to eat before heading toward our next stop.

Ayutthaya was a city that at one time was home to lavish palaces and Buddhist temples. Now only ruins remained, though they, too, were a sight to be seen. Piles of red clay bricks lay beside partial structures and fragments of statues. Julie and I climbed the rubble to the top of one structure, overlooking the ancient city. Beside the ruins was the Ayutthaya Elephant Palace, where you could feed and ride the elephants. Julie and I bought bunches of bananas, waiting in line to feed the giant, majestic animals. Julie transformed into a young child, filled with excitement, squealing as two elephants wrapped their trunks around her in an embrace—a shameless act, really, as they reached behind her for more bananas. Still, it was the first time since Robby died that I saw her truly let go and allow herself to be happy.

Julie barely looked up from her phone during the long drive back to the hotel. From the side, I could see the videos that she had taken at the floating markets and of the elephants playing on her small screen.

"What are you doing?" I asked.

"Making a video," she responded.

We arrived at the hotel, exhausted, each falling onto our beds. Julie fell asleep instantly. I took out my phone, searching Facebook and Instagram to pass the time. I saw that Julie had posted her video, complete with special effects and music. She chose a song called "W.A.Y.S.," which played as images of our trip flashed by— its lyrics saying everything:

> *An angel walked up to my door*
> *Opened the windows to my soul*
> *Told me he thinks that I should know*
> *That life only gets harder*
> *But you gotta get stronger*
> *This is for my brother . . .*

Chapter 18

24

It was April 1 in Indonesia, but still March 31 in America. I decided to recognize the American calendar so I could hold off on facing the reality of the day: Robby's birthday.

He would have been 24. Just 24.

He would have been a full-time employee at Genentech. We would have been going out for a nice dinner somewhere, or maybe I would have cooked something at home and invited people over.

On his 23rd birthday, I covered our dining table with cut-up panels of brown paper bags. I made a feast of crab, shrimp, corn on the cob and hot link sausages in a spicy garlic sauce—a recipe I tried to replicate from one of his favorite restaurants. By the time we were done, the table was covered in fragments of crab, shrimp shells and stripped corncobs. Robby was covered in hot sauce. He rubbed his belly, as he often did after a big meal.

"Thanks, Mom. That was good!" he said, before heading out to celebrate his birthday with some friends.

Maybe he would have met someone special by now, and she would have been with us. Maybe she would have become my daughter-in-law someday, and the mother of his children. Maybe they'd have a boy and a girl, like I did. I would cook for her and

Robby and help with the baby as she recovered from giving birth. But I would be respectful of their space—not meddling or intrusive—at least that's what I told myself. Maybe he would have bought his own boat, bringing his young family on sailing trips around the San Francisco Bay. Maybe.

As Julie flew home from Thailand, Cicero flew in to meet me in Indonesia. This would be the busiest leg of my trip, but I cleared Robby's birthday so we could make the one-hour flight to Bali. I had never been there, but I knew it was steeped in Hinduism, which Robby had also been studying, and that it was far from the bustling streets of Jakarta, where all my meetings were.

Bali was unlike any place I had ever been, filled with lush vegetation, stunning rice terraces, long stretches of white sandy beaches, mesmerizing sunsets and unencumbered views of the famous Bali moon. I was in paradise—and yet I was in hell. I wasn't haunted by memories of Robby; I was haunted by all the "maybes"—visions of what he might have been. And on the morning of his birthday, all I could think of was what he might have been doing on this day. What he would have accomplished during his 24th year on this Earth. What he would have become beyond 24.

I wanted to draw the curtains, leave the lights off, pull the blankets over my head and stay this way until his birthday was over. Instead, Cicero and I walked to the beach to watch the sunrise. We wrote his name in large letters on the sand, as if it were our SOS to him. *We're here. Please help us. Save us.*

I found an empty bamboo structure overlooking the ocean, and I climbed up and sat in meditation pose. While Cicero took pictures from afar, I closed my eyes and tried to meditate. The question kept popping into my head: *What would you do if you were here?* It was in asking this question that I found my answer to how we should spend his birthday. Not by being sad or staying in the room. But by doing all the things Robby would have done if he were here with us. And with Robby, that meant doing *everything*.

"If you're going to do something, you might as well get the most out of it," he'd say. "No fear."

I called the concierge to arrange for a driver for the entire day, stopping everywhere and signing up for everything we thought Robby would have enjoyed. We dipped our hands in the holy waters of Pura Gunung Kawi, an ancient Hindu temple that was located in a ravine between rice fields. We walked the breathtaking grounds, passing cool blue pools of holy water and taking in the ancient ruins surrounded by Hindu statues and artifacts. Our driver then drove us to the top of a steep ridge where we had a stunning panoramic view of the Tegalalang Rice Terrace, which from our vantage point looked like wavy ripples embossed on an endless expanse of green velvet. We lunched on the balcony of a restaurant that sat atop a high mountain overlooking an active volcano. Robby hated shopping, but he loved local crafts and cultural souvenirs, so we walked through the colorful stalls in Ubud manned by local artisans selling their wares. We hiked up a narrow path in a rainforest to witness the making of Indonesia's famous Kopi Luwak, the most expensive coffee in the world.

"What?" Robby asked animatedly when I first brought home a bag from my last trip to Indonesia. "It comes from *where*?"

I explained that Indonesian coffee farmers gathered the feces from civet cats, where they would then "retrieve" the whole and partial cherry coffee beans that were eaten and defecated by the animal. Something about the digestive process was believed to make the coffee one of the best—if not *the* best—in the world. Robby scratched his head as he decided whether he could really follow through with his "no fear" mantra. "So should I make you a cup?" I asked. "I . . . guess?" he responded, though he was less interested in how the coffee tasted than he was in the process itself. We went straight to the source, knowing he would have jumped at the chance.

"This is the civet cat," said our guide. I could barely make out the small, dark cat, snuggled in a little cave. He showed us how the beans were sterilized and roasted. A slight woman sat hunched over a large, wok-shaped pan, swirling and tossing the beans around. It was a rather primitive manufacturing process for a product that was the most expensive of its kind in the world.

It was nearly sunset when we reached our last stop with our driver at the Sacred Monkey Forest Sanctuary, home to a Hindu temple that was run according to the Hindu principle of Tri Hita Karana, or "three ways to reach spiritual and physical well-being."

The "three ways" referred to three relationships people needed to live harmoniously during their lives: humans and humans, humans and the natural environment, and humans and "The Supreme God"—or any higher entity the person recognized. For me, it was the Universe. It was the place I thought Robby would have most loved, as he was clearly following some kind of spiritual path before he was killed. I felt I had taken the baton, continuing along the same mysterious and wondrous journey.

We returned to the hotel in time for dinner. Down the road there was an open-air restaurant and bar. A local reggae band was on stage, transitioning effortlessly from one Bob Marley song to the next: *Don't worry about a thing/'Cause every little thing gonna be all right.* We tipped our waiter 313,800 rupiah, the equivalent of 24 U.S. dollars, more than the meal itself, to mark what would have been Robby's 24th birthday.

I signed the receipt: "Thank you, from Robby."

It was raining heavily the day we were set to fly back to Jakarta. I checked the airline website that morning to see if the flight was canceled, but it was still scheduled to depart on time. We had been in flight for about 40 minutes, just about 10 minutes before we were supposed to land, when the aircraft was shaken by turbulence. I looked out at the dark clouds and the rainwater streaming down the oval window of the small plane, as if we were going through a carwash. The pilot made an announcement in Indonesian as the "fasten seatbelts" sign flashed on. The flight attendants scurried down the aisle from the back of the plane where they had been collecting garbage and into their seats facing us, strapping themselves in tightly.

The aircraft began its descent, submerging itself in the stormy clouds that now darkened the whole cabin. And then the whole plane began to shake. Passengers were screaming "Allah!" An older woman behind me was now sobbing as her body shook violently against her seat belt. People took out their cellphones and began texting, as if saying goodbye to their loved ones. I squeezed Cicero's hand, both of us remaining quiet but tense.

We felt the plane turn sharply upward again, emerging from the clouds and into the clear skies. It was evident we couldn't land. But what now?

"How long can we stay up here?" I asked Cicero, knowing he was just as clueless as I was. I knew we would have to land at some point, and that we would need to go back through the stormy weather. I felt a moment of panic—and then a moment of peace.

What if the plane crashes and this is my last day on Earth? I thought. *If I die here, I will be with Robby.*

The thought of it made me happy, imagining him meeting me on the other side. And then I thought of Julie, still left behind, losing both of us. I was the mother of two, each child belonging in a different world, and I was torn between wanting to join one while still being there for the other.

The pilot landed the plane in a remote airport, about an hour away from the original destination. I saw Cicero wipe his forehead with his napkin, letting out a deep breath. Women were sobbing around us, calling their loved ones and detailing the ordeal. Cicero put his arm around me and gave me a reassuring squeeze, though I didn't need it. In that moment, I wasn't afraid to die. Because it would bring me to my son.

～

"Oh, my God, are you okay?" Phill Fullon asked as we sat in the back of the taxi. Phill was my colleague based in Manila, who attended meetings with me whenever I was in the Philippines. He placed his hand over mine as I gasped for air and felt my chest tighten.

There was nothing unusual about this cab ride. I knew all drivers in Southeast Asia drove in the same manic, car-weaving, signs-and-pedestrians-be-damned fashion. I also knew that it worked for them. No matter how chaotic it seemed to me, they all seemed to anticipate each other's moves on the road, like the synchronicity of a flock of birds. I'd been in countless taxis in this region over the years. And yet, I was having my first panic attack in months as the driver vacillated between speeding up and braking hard, squeezing into the slightest of spaces, allowing me to practically smell the breath of the passenger in the car beside us as we inched our way through Manila's infamously clogged Epifanio de los Santos Avenue. Or as locals commonly referred to it: "damned EDSA."

The panic began with my heart rate speeding up, followed by my breathing, then the tightening of my chest, then the perspiration. It didn't take long for Phill to see something was wrong.

"What can I do? What's wrong?"

I focused on breathing, ignoring him completely. When the car came to a stop I was dizzy. I felt the familiar tingling sensation radiating through my limbs, and I was now covered in a cold sweat.

"Just wait," I said, to no one in particular, before I opened the door to get out. I caught my breath and wiped my face with a paper towel from my bag. I realized then what had caused the attack. The erratic driving brought me back to the drive we made through traffic after we got the call that Robby had been shot. The freeway was congested, and Cicero tried everything he could, driving along the shoulder and squeezing between cars to get through. It was a trigger for my PTSD.

"So," said Phill, as I finally got out of the car, "I have some weed at home. Want some?" We both looked at each other before I let out a laugh. I couldn't help it. He looked relieved, wiping the sweat from his own forehead now. "Shit. What *was* that? Never mind. Let's just finish our meetings and get a drink."

Later that evening, we sat on lounge chairs by the hotel pool, drinking our bottles of San Miguel beer. I told him what had caused the panic attack, initiating the first conversation we had about Robby and everything that had happened. He sat quietly, listening to the whole story.

"You know," he began. He paused for a while before continuing, and I knew he was being extra cautious before proceeding. "I know that this is considered a third-world country. And I know that the Philippines has its problems and that we are a poor country. But we don't shoot our children in classrooms. We don't kill each other in movie theaters. We're a third-world country, but we don't do that."

This was during Benigno Aquino III's presidency, before the Philippines came under international scrutiny for alleged extra-judicial killings perpetrated during his successor Rodrigo Duterte's administration.

But I knew what Phill was trying to convey. And it was something I had thought of during the whole trip. Despite my initial nervousness before my presentation in Bangkok and the one panic attack during our taxi ride through Manila, I realized that the loud noises and hectic crowds of Asia did not cause me any anxiety. Thailand was under military rule after months of political protests led to a coup in May 2014. After the country's army chief publicly declared that the military had seized power, he declared himself prime minister. Even as I met with members of their national government, it was uncertain that our work would go anywhere because of the threat of further political unrest. And even then, I felt more safe in this country than I did in my own.

Despite what Marsha and I had discussed during my therapy sessions, it wasn't crowds and loud noises that triggered my panic attacks—it was crowds and loud noises *in my community*. My community, where Robby was killed. My community, where the killers might still be. I didn't feel safe in crowds near my home because the person ringing up my groceries could be the person who shot my son. The person delivering a package to my home could have knowledge of what happened and yet remained silent for fear of retribution.

Here, I was cloaked in anonymity. Here, guns and stories of mass shootings weren't everywhere—on TV shows, commercials, the news—being administered like shock therapy on my already-tattered nerves. Here, no one was connected to my son's unsolved murder.

It was at that moment that I considered moving away. Away from Vallejo. Away from California and the United States. We could start over, bringing with us our beautiful memories of Robby, while leaving behind all the painful memories of what took him away from us. Despite all the progress we had made in our healing process, I knew that the prospects of arrests and a trial were still looming. It was not over.

And when I returned home, I realized that it was really just beginning.

Part Two

Part Two

Anger

Chapter 19

One Year

"Look! Look at what the ocean gave me!" Robby yelled as he swam onto shore holding up a large coconut that he found in the water. It was my birthday, and we spent the day on Kailua Beach in Oahu, Hawaii. It was a far cry from the tourist-dense beaches in Waikiki. Kailua was on the east side of the island, with white, powdery sand and ocean waters that showcased an ombré of blues—a translucent turquoise bordering the shoreline, transitioning gradually to a deep sapphire the farther away from shore you swam. Many days there were only a few people dotting the beach, and it felt like our own private retreat. Robby plopped himself on the sand, bending over with a rock and his newly found treasure from the ocean. "Here, for you," he said, handing it over to me. On the side of the coconut he had carved out a message using the sharp edge of a rock: *Happy birthday, Mom.*

We went to that beach every time we went to Oahu, stopping by the local market to buy an assortment of Hawaiian *poke* (a raw fish salad mostly made with tuna), taro chips and bottles of ice-cold Waialua pineapple soda. I'd spread everything out on our straw mats on the sand while Robby and Julie swam until sunset. It was his favorite place to go.

This is where I wanted to be on the one-year anniversary of his death. A place where he had spent so many lazy, palm-tree-swaying days just laughing, relaxing and being carefree. I arranged for ukulele players and singers to play his favorite Hawaiian music by the popular, local singer Israel "Iz" Kamakawiwoʻole—"White Sandy Beach" and his versions of "Somewhere Over the Rainbow" and "What a Wonderful World." Following Hawaiian tradition, there would be a blowing of the *pu,* or the conch shell, to mark both the beginning and the end of the ceremony. I ordered trays of Robby's favorite local foods: kalua pork, chicken long rice, lomi-lomi salmon and lau lau. It was difficult to find food Robby *didn't* like, so that part was easy. We would have a moment of silence at the precise time Robby died, then we would each break our leis, pulling the fresh orchids from the strings and throwing the fuchsia and purple blooms into the ocean, sending our love and messages to Robby along with them. Ten family members were going, and I rented a large vacation home near Kailua Beach that would accommodate all of us. I called Cora to see if she wanted to meet us for the ceremony. "Of course," she responded when I told her about our plans to mark the one-year anniversary. "I wouldn't miss it."

I went over my checklist: vacation rental, leis, food, ukulele players, rental car. We had one week left before our flight, and I wanted to make sure everything was taken care of. We were all anxious to get away—far away from the place that only a year prior threatened to break us, individually and as a family. One year later and we were stronger. We had bonded together for strength, and we focused on healing rather than revenge.

Following Robby's interests continued to be a bittersweet journey for me. I learned more about him as I experienced what he experienced. I wished that we had done these things together while he still lived—though part of me believed he was with me the whole way. And now, we were creating our own rituals.

Returning to his favorite beach, watching the sunset and marking the day together was just another step in our healing.

"I'm going to go to the store to buy some last-minute stuff for Hawaii," I told Cicero as I walked into our room.

"Okay," he said, looking up from his laptop. I was grabbing my purse from the closet when our home phone started to ring. I reached to answer, purse in hand, ready to cut the conversation short, no matter who it was.

"I'm looking for Pati Poblete," the man said.

"This is she," I replied.

"This is Detective Mason. I've been working on your son's case."

My heart began racing.

"I'm calling to let you know three arrests were made late last night. There's a fourth suspect on the run. We'd like to meet with you and Robby's father."

I heard a thud on the ground and realized I had dropped my purse. I took a seat on the bench at the foot of our bed.

"Ms. Poblete?"

I couldn't respond.

"My partner and I would like to meet with you so we can give you a full update."

Cicero was standing in front of me now, his brow furrowed with concern. "What?" he mouthed.

"We can meet you in two hours," the detective said. "We'll see you then."

I hung up the phone, covering my face and crying into my palms. "What happened? Who was that?" Cicero asked.

"They caught them," I cried. "They caught them."

One year later.

They caught them.

Julie, Ruben, Cicero and I were sitting across from the two detectives at the glass dining table in Ruben's house. I recognized the dark-haired detective from the night Robby was killed. He was the one asking us questions. I didn't recognize the other guy, Detective Mason, who had blond hair and a larger build. It was he who told us what they knew, in robotic, matter-of-fact statements, while the dark-haired detective scanned our faces intensely, looking for reactions, clues, any inkling that we may be hiding anything.

We were told there were four suspects involved in Robby's killing. The three were arrested separately, all in Vallejo. The district attorney thought there was enough evidence to push forward with the arrests. No witnesses were willing to come forward at the time, even though it happened in daylight at a busy intersection. There was one witness who sustained a head injury as the suspects fled the scene, but there was no guarantee he would testify. There was a surveillance tape from a local business that captured grainy images of the suspects driving into the parking lot, and then speeding away after gunshots are heard on the audio. It was an attempted robbery. It wasn't random. It was targeted. He was shot multiple times, in the neck, chest and arms. The weapon was never found.

They read us the names of the suspects and their ages, one by one, looking at us after each name was read. I didn't recognize any of them, until the last suspect's name. Cora's nephew. My friend who had been so supportive, who was going to meet us in one week in Hawaii for Robby's anniversary. I remember her telling me about her nephew before, though I never knew him personally. Robby had met him years ago in high school through a mutual friend, though they never became good friends. This was him. He was among those arrested, and he was the lead suspect in the case. My head was spinning. I didn't know how to make sense of it all. I disclosed the link to one of the detectives as they took notes. "I know his aunt," I said. "She's one of my best friends. She's my daughter's godmother. She was in my wedding."

"Should we cancel our travel plans?" I asked. "It's almost Robby's one-year anniversary, and we were all going to go to Hawaii to have a ceremony for him."

Detective Mason's body language changed. He put his report down on the table, relaxed his shoulders and leaned forward, making eye contact with me. "I've dealt with a lot of families," he said. "What I want to say to you, to all of you, is this: They've taken away too much. Don't miss one birthday, one wedding, one anniversary, one trip. Live your life. They have taken too much from you already. You can't let them take the rest of your lives."

I went home and picked up the phone. I didn't know if the arrests would be in the news the next day, and I wanted to talk to Cora before that happened.

"Hi, Pati!" she answered cheerily, seeing my number pop up on her cellphone.

I opened my mouth to speak but no words came out. I cried deeply and sorrowfully, picturing the trial. Her family on one side, ours on the other. She was used to picking up the phone and hearing this same sound. She spent hours sitting on the line with me. "Just let it out," she'd say. "I'm here. I'm here."

She did the same now. "Just let it out."

"Cora, they made the arrests," I said.

"Oh, honey," she sighed. "I know it's hard, but that's a good thing. Now they're off the streets. You can find closure. You can start to heal."

"But Cora, it's your nephew," I said. "It's your nephew." I was crying too much now. I couldn't answer her questions.

"What?" she asked. "What do you mean? My nephew? Oh, my God!" She was crying now, too. We both could barely hear each other over our own cries of anguish.

"I wanted to tell you before it came out because I wanted to tell you that it doesn't change anything between us," I said. "We're still friends. We're still sisters, and you are still welcome to meet us in Hawaii."

After hearing this she let out a long cry. "How can I face your family? All this time I've been watching you suffer and in pain. And now I know it was at the hands of my own family. Oh, Pati. Oh, my God. I don't understand. I don't understand."

We stayed on the phone for nearly an hour. Neither one of us saying a word. Just crying into the phone at the cruel irony of it all. It was a tragedy that rivaled any Shakespearean plot.

"You are still welcome, but I understand if you don't come," I finally said.

"I don't know if I can," she responded. "But thank you for telling me yourself and saying that our friendship won't change. Thank you so much for that."

We hung up, and I continued to sit, staring at the phone for hours. I knew that I was being naive. Of course our friendship would change. It was already changed forever.

Chapter 20

White Sandy Beach

We collected our bags from the baggage claim at Honolulu Airport—Julie, Cicero, Ruben and I. My cousin and her family arrived a day earlier and were already settled into the vacation home we rented on the eastern part of Oahu. My brother would be joining us in a couple of days.

"Let's go to the car rental office," I said. I had reserved an SUV, knowing we would be traveling in large groups. Cicero, Ruben and I approached the counter.

"You all gonna be drivers, yah?" the woman asked in a thick Hawaiian pidgin accent.

I looked to Cicero on my left, then to Ruben on my right. "Yah," we responded.

"I need your driver's licenses then," she said. We reached for our wallets, handing them to her one by one. "Oh, you get discount because you two married," she said, pointing to Ruben and me. We both still had the same last name. After the divorce, I chose to keep it because I wanted the same surname as my children.

"Uh, actually," I said, "he is my ex-husband. And he is my fiancé," I said, pointing to Cicero. Her eyes grew wide.

"Oh. Dis no Utah over he-ah!"

I didn't understand. I looked at Ruben and then to Cicero. *Oh,* Utah, I thought, *as in Mormons. As in polygamy.* The light bulb seemed to turn on above our heads at the same time, because we were all nervously laughing now, realizing how confusing it may have seemed from the outside. I felt the heat in my cheeks. "Please, car rental lady, let me explain," I wanted to pull her aside and say. But where would I even begin? No, this wasn't Utah; it was far more complicated than that.

                            ∽

We pulled up to an area at the far end of Kailua Beach, where the caterers and musicians said they would meet us. I saw some tables and chairs already propped up against a tree. The table covers were flapping as the trade winds blew, and I used our bags and a framed picture of Robby to weigh them down. I had been keeping busy since we arrived in Hawaii, ordering and picking up leis at Cindy's Lei and Flower Shoppe, a local favorite in Honolulu's Chinatown district, meeting with the caterers and making sure everything was set, giving a list of songs I wanted the ukulele players to sing. But today was September 21, 2015, and nothing more could be done but remember Robby.

The day before we left for the trip, I received another call from Detective Mason, letting me know that the fourth arrest was made. At the time, I was at the Westfield San Francisco Centre, a nine-story bustling mall at the heart of downtown San Francisco. I had just come from a business meeting and decided to pick up some food to bring home. Standing in the massive food emporium between the Korean and Mediterranean stalls, I felt my cellphone buzzing in my purse. "Hello?" I answered.

"Pati, Detective Mason. Just wanted to let you know we made the fourth arrest this morning." They found the suspect in Richmond,

California, about 20 minutes from Vallejo. Now all four of them were in custody, and they could move forward with their arraignments and legal proceedings. I thanked him for letting me know and for all his hard work on the case, hanging up the phone and heading straight for the bakery in an attempt to drown my anxiety with a case of cream puffs.

I couldn't think about any of that now. I went around distributing the leis, placing them around each person's neck—Ruben, Cicero, Julie, my brother and cousins. I spotted four men with their instruments, and another carrying over trays of food to the tables. I waved them over.

"Maybe we should put the tables in there," the man with the food yelled. "In case it might rain later." The weather was warm, but I knew Hawaiian rains came and went, from downpour to tropical sun, in an instant. Cicero, Ruben and I walked over to help them move the tables and chairs under one of the wooden structures along the beach that looked like mini pavilions. The caterers brought the trays out of their van one by one as the musicians stood in the corner, testing tunes on their ukuleles and harmonizing.

I walked toward the beach, wanting a moment to myself. I stopped when I reached the water, feeling its warmth wash over my feet and causing them to sink into the moist, comforting sand. I imagined Robby coming back from the water holding a coconut over his head.

"Pati!" I heard a faint voice coming from a distance. I turned in the direction of the call and saw a slight figure, long hair blowing in the wind. It was Cora. I walked toward her and we met in the middle, stopping to scan each other's faces before engaging in a long, meaningful hug. At this moment, there was nothing left to say between us. Despite everything, I wanted her there. Despite everything, she showed up.

I led her to the rest of the family, seeing her hesitation. Though she was completely blameless, I knew she felt shame—just as I had felt shame when Robby was killed. I understood it, and I knew that she was in extreme pain because of it. Shame can be just as debilitating as grief itself. It robs you of your confidence and any feeling of worth. You are minimized to whatever it is you feel shame about, and your instinct is to crawl and hide. Your instinct is to lower your eyes, avoid eye contact, bow your head, slouch your back. As if all those actions could somehow transform you into an invisible ball that can roll away into oblivion. Your body language says, "Please don't look at me," because at that moment, you can't stand to look at yourself or face whatever action you think represents you. Shame is suffering.

⤳

I saw you in my dream/We were walking hand in hand/On a white sandy beach of Hawaii.

"Don't you know any other lines?" Julie groaned. Robby had been singing the same line from Iz's "White Sandy Beach" the whole day. We were in the car now, driving back from the beach. He let out a giggle and started to sing again: *I saw you in my dream/We were walking hand in hand/On a white sandy beach of Hawaii.*

By now we were all groaning, Cicero, Julie and I. "Make it stop!" I yelled. He was on an endless loop, seemingly taking pleasure in annoying all of us. But he kept going, stretching that line into one never-ending song. By the end of that day, we never wanted to hear that song again. And yet on this day, it was the only song that could have brought us comfort.

It was slightly overcast when the ceremony began on the beach. One of the musicians stood by the water, holding the conch shell in both hands and blowing into it, sending the horn sound through the air, the winds carrying it off into the water. We each removed the leis from our necks, snapping the strings and pulling the flowers off. We cast them into the ocean waters at the same time, each of us crying and sending our own messages to Robby in silence. Just as Cicero and I had done in Bali, we wrote Robby's name in the sand in large letters. We stood side by side with our arms around each other behind his name as Cora took our picture. One of the musicians stood next to her with another camera, capturing the moment, both sweet and somber. We returned to the pavilion where Robby's favorite foods sat ready, smoke rising from the trays. At the head of the table was Robby's framed picture on a small easel. It was a picture cropped from our last family portrait. He was wearing a black, short-sleeve polo shirt, standing with his arms folded and a huge grin on his face. With his bulky arms and pulled-back hair, he resembled the genie in *Aladdin*. We all laughed as someone made the observation. We settled into our chairs at the long table to eat as the musicians sang:

> *I saw you in my dream*
> *We were walking hand in hand*
> *On a white sandy beach of Hawaii*
>
> *We were playing in the sun*
> *We were having so much fun*
> *On a white sandy beach of Hawaii*
>
> *The sound of the ocean*
> *Soothes my restless soul*
> *The sound of the ocean*
> *Rocks me all night long*

Those hot long summer days
Lying there in the sun
On a white sandy beach of Hawaii

The sound of the ocean
Soothes my restless soul
The sound of the ocean
Rocks me all night long

Last night in my dream
I saw your face again
We were there in the sun
On a white sandy beach of Hawaii

There, I thought. *You finally know the rest of the song.*

Ruben pulled Cora aside after we ate, as I had asked him to do. "Tell her it's okay," I said. I saw her lower her head and cover her face with both hands. Her shoulders shook and I knew she was crying. Ruben put his arms around her, reassuring her that no one blamed her for anything and that nothing had changed. "You and Pati have been friends for a long time," he said. "She knows you love her, and she knows what you have done for her."

"I just can't believe it," she cried, trying to stop her tears. "I'm so sorry."

She stayed up until the last minute, leaving just enough time for herself to drive to the airport, return her rental car and catch her flight back home to Maui. "We'll talk more," I said, before saying goodbye. I watched her drive off, feeling hopeful and anxious about the future of our friendship.

When we returned to the vacation rental, we all gathered at the dining table, sending one another the photos from the day through our smartphones. "Look at this," Ruben said. We looked at the group photo of us standing by Robby's name, one taken by Cora, and the other taken by one of the musicians who was standing next to her. In the first photo his name could be clearly seen in the sand. In the other photo, there was a bright swath of light where his name should have been, illuminating the foreground and reflecting partially on our bodies. We went through all the possible explanations. The sky was overcast at the time we took the photo, and we knew it couldn't be a reflection of the sun. And both pictures were taken at the same time, from the same angle.

"He wants us to know he was there," I said.

⤳

On our last day in Hawaii I sent Cora a text message, hoping it could help both of us as we struggled to understand everything. We hadn't spoken since the ceremony.

September 27, 2015, 12:57 p.m.

Cora, sorry I didn't get to text you last night; it got too late. We're getting ready to leave soon.

What I wanted to say is that, like you, I have been thinking a lot about what has happened, what is happening now, and what possible lesson there could be in all of it. The irony is not lost on me that the person who has helped me so much, and has shown me so much compassion throughout my grief is related to the person involved in causing me so much pain.

When Robby was killed my faith in humanity, in God, in fairness, in life itself was so shattered. All I could see was darkness and I couldn't see through my loss and pain. Why would anyone take my son away?

And then something unexpected happened. The community rallied. I saw people I haven't seen in years. People cried with me;

strangers offered donations. So much love and kindness helped to carry us through. And there was you.

What I have taken away from this may seem so simple, but is so profound to me. The world is filled with darkness, ignorance and hate—those are what took Robby away. But I have been shown that the universe is full of love, compassion and light. It can be so easy for me to channel my grief into anger and vengeance. But I choose to emulate the light and the goodness that I have been shown.

Someone in your family was part of taking Robby away. But someone in your family—you—has helped heal my heart. That's the balance of the universe—the dark and the light. And it's up to each of us to decide what path we follow.

Chapter 21

Someone to Blame

Cicero and I were preparing to leave the house to pick up my car from a routine maintenance check. I woke up angry that morning, as I had done many mornings since we returned from Hawaii. Now that I was no longer preoccupied with making arrangements for our trip and the memorial ceremony, I was left to process the arrests and the details the detectives shared with us. Cicero mentioned that his family was having a barbecue that day. *Maybe we could pick up my car and head straight over?*

It was the last thing I wanted to do. I didn't want to be around anyone, let alone at a family barbecue where everyone would be laughing and enjoying themselves. I held my tongue. Cicero had done nothing but support all of us—me, Julie, my mom. He had become close to Ruben and his whole family. The least I could do was go to his family's barbecue. But I was seething inside. *Why would he even expect me to go? Can't he see I'm in no shape to chow down on ribs and corn?*

I remained quiet on the freeway, turning my head to face the window, staring aimlessly at the stream of passing buildings and trees. Dreading the rest of the day and wondering how I could possibly fake being happy.

"You don't have to go. I'll just go," Cicero said, breaking the silence. But I could see he was upset.

"It's not that I don't want to be with your family," I tried to explain. "I feel anxiety. I don't want to be around anyone."

He looked straight ahead, with a rare look that told me this would become an argument if I pushed it—and I did. As we neared the exit, I was screaming as loudly as I could, "You don't understand! The last thing I want to do is go to a party!"

"Just once," he said, "I wish you could be there for me."

I knew he was right, but it was too late to push pause. In my mind, I was already fast-forwarding to a life alone. *I don't need him*, I told myself. *I need to grieve in peace without the expectations and pressures of a relationship. It will be easier without him.* I continued to say things that I knew I'd regret, and by the time we reached the dealership where my car was, I all but told him it was over. He drove off, and I turned with a huff, entering the building.

"Pati! Great to see you. Your car's all ready." I took the keys from the car dealer's hands, forcing a smile, as if bombs weren't exploding all around me.

The blowup was weeks, if not months, in the making. Because Robby was killed the very day we set our wedding plans, I avoided any talk of getting married. I questioned whether we should even be together anymore and if Robby's death wasn't the ultimate bad omen. Our wedding would forever be linked to the day Robby was killed, and I couldn't bring myself to even think about getting married anymore. I took my engagement ring off, placed it back in its black velvet box and into a drawer where it sat with uncertainty of ever re-emerging. "But I asked Robby if I could marry you," Cicero said one day. "And he said yes. He wanted us to get married."

I didn't respond, and it never came up again.

After we returned from Hawaii, Detective Mason contacted me

a few more times, giving me updates and asking questions. The majority of the evidence was against Suspect 1, whom he described numerous times as the "mastermind" of the whole thing. In fact, it wasn't clear whether the other three even knew Robby at all, but they knew where he would be because of Suspect 1, and they were sent to carry out an armed robbery.

In the end, Suspects 2, 3 and 4 drove away with nothing, not one dollar.

For weeks after hearing these details, I would go into my home office, shut the door and just sit, feeling the blood rush to my head, setting off a painful pulsing against my skull and behind my eyes. My heart would start beating irregularly—stopping, then sputtering, like the engine of an old car, fighting for just a few more miles of life. I'd take in a deep breath through my nose, exhaling through my mouth, as I had learned in yoga. I closed my eyes and counted my breaths as I had learned at the monastery. But nothing was working. The notion of forgiveness was much easier when I didn't know whom I was forgiving. It was much easier to accept that he was gone when I didn't know how needlessly and ruthlessly he died. How could I apply everything I had learned in the past year when I felt so much anger toward these four men?

I thought of their mothers, wondering if they knew what their sons had done to mine. I thought of Cora and the family I had watched with admiration during her wedding. Her sister sitting in her cream dress in the front row—this was her son. Her parents, who sent me a sympathy card with a check for $100 after Robby was killed. Did they know now it was their grandson who did this?

"Each of them have records," Detective Mason told me. "They've been in and out of trouble for a long time."

"But my son was trying to do something with his life," I said, not knowing why I was saying this to him.

I began smoking cigarettes and feeding my rage with unhealthy amounts of food. I was in full self-sabotage mode. Before Robby's death I was exercising regularly, alternating between cardio and lifting weights. "I can see your arms are getting toned," Robby said one day during breakfast, shortly before he died. That all went away.

I stopped going to the gym because of my anxiety and ceased all forms of exercise, purposely letting myself go. I went on tirades, telling Cicero the suspects were nothing but "pieces of shit." They had long records; my son did not. And yet he was the one who died.

Why?

I would replay everything in my mind until I grew dizzy. My blood pressure elevated to alarming levels. I shut down all my social media accounts. The last thing I needed to see were pictures of my friends with their smiling children. Their families intact, mocking me. Cicero and I began arguing more and more as I misdirected my rage toward him. With all the progress I had made, I was right back to where I started, only now I felt something I had not yet felt: anger. I began feeling paranoid about Cora. Though I didn't blame her for anything, I knew that no matter what, this was her blood. Anything I told her about the case may be repeated to Suspect 1's parents—her sister and former brother-in-law. I knew she wouldn't betray my trust intentionally, but I couldn't take a chance. I sent her a text:

Sept. 28, 2015, 1:43 p.m.

Sorry, I'm not comfortable talking to you anymore. I'm not mad at you, I'm just very afraid.

She responded:

Jesus. It's getting so complicated. If you need to cut me off, I understand. I'll miss you.

Nearly a year would pass before we spoke again. I reached out to her as the date for the preliminary hearing was set. I thought of how I would feel seeing her parents and siblings on the other side of the courtroom—much different circumstances than when I last saw them at her wedding. And then I had an overwhelming need to reach out to her, after months of silence between us. I went on her Facebook page, scrolling through her posts and pictures. Her daughter smiling. She and her husband on the beach. School events. I sent her a private message, which remained unanswered for almost a week.

And then finally, I got a response:

AUG 10 2016

Hi Pati! I was so nervous to open your email. As time went on, I was feeling unsure about how you feel about me. I was so relieved to hear it. It's crazy because I've been thinking about you a lot, too, and as the days were passing, I felt less and less connected. I also wasn't sure the extent to which you want to limit our contact so I've not even tried.

We resumed our communication and made a conscious effort to make sense of everything and find a joint purpose through our tragic bond. But it took nearly a year after hearing the details of the case for me to get to that point.

For now, I could only feel rage.

I went to my therapy session, unleashing it all as Marsha adjusted her glasses and creased her brow in concern. It was a side of me she hadn't seen before. I could barely contain my anger. All the healing, the Zen, the forgiveness were out the door. I knew who was responsible now. I knew greed and betrayal were the cause, and while I still didn't seek revenge, I was not prepared to deal with the fury that now consumed me. It was easier to seek peace when I was in the dark, and I wished with all my heart that I never learned the details.

PSYCHOTHERAPY NOTE
  *CHIEF COMPLAINT:
  Pati D Poblete is a 45 Y female who returned to focus on addressing symptoms involving: depression
  anxiety
  sleep disturbance
  grief
  relationship problems
  *Updated Clinical Status/Relevant History/Active Abuse-Trauma Concerns/Treatment Response:
  Pati reports she and partner had an argument and 'he left for a week'. Fight was about attending a family party. He did return but Pati reports that she realized she could manage on her own if needed. Pati reports now 4 people have been arrested. She reports increased anxiety, increased compulsive eating and more weight gain, she works most of the time at home in her pajamas and only goes out if necessary. She has had to discontinue relationship with a close friend due to ties with the family of whose son [was involved in her son's death], unable to speak freely with people she had been close to prior to the arrests. Pati reports sleep erratic, onset insomnia and sleep 4–5 hours/night several times per week since the arrests.
  Social withdrawal, inability to enjoy herself with others, panic attacks when driving alone at night when she gets sweaty. Session explores ways to address anxiety and depression as Pati expects lengthy trial during the upcoming year.

Cicero returned home after a week, during which I had not seen or heard from him. I was in my office when I heard him come in. I heard his dresser drawers open and close, and I was convinced he was picking up the rest of his belongings. I continued working on my computer, as if I didn't care. I couldn't deal with more heartbreak. But then the sounds stopped, and after a while I wondered if and when he would leave. I walked over to our room and found him standing by the window, looking out into the backyard.

"How are you?" he said, as if we had not gone through everything we had gone through together.

"Fine," I said, with an iciness in my tone. In my mind, I was done. I was ready to let him go because I had already let so much go.

"What do you want to do?" he said. I told him I realized while he was away that I could do this alone. That perhaps I had been depending on him too much, and it was time for me to stand on my own.

"You don't have to feel guilty or obligated," I said. "I will be okay." I looked at him as I said this, and I knew this wasn't what he expected. "What do you want?" I said.

"I keep thinking about everything, and all I know is that we are best friends," he answered. It wasn't what I expected to hear either. I was self-destructing, pushing everyone away—and no matter what, he stayed. I realized that I was pushing him away because I felt guilt. Guilt that we were looking at wedding sites during my son's last living day. Guilt that I could even fathom a happy future after such a tragedy. Guilt that I was still here to share a life with someone who loved me, while my son would never get that chance.

Chapter 22

It Just Is

"I don't have a plan to kill myself, but I don't want to live."

I was sitting across from Marsha, slouching, with my head down. I never had suicidal thoughts because I could never do that to Julie, but I regretted every morning I woke up. And since hearing the details of the case, I hadn't been able to get back on the path toward healing that I thought I was on. There were times during that first year when friends and family members would express their anger about Robby's killing, but I shunned it. I had built a bubble around myself. Grief, anxiety, depression, love, sympathy. These were all acceptable feelings. The only anger I allowed myself to feel was toward God—because it was easier. It was like blaming the universe and deciding that life was just unfair. It wasn't a clear target. I shielded myself from anger toward the suspects because I knew that rage, vengeance and hate would soon follow. I knew that once I allowed myself to be angry, it could completely take over, clouding my judgment and setting a destructive course for the rest of our lives. I would not allow myself to feel that anger— until now.

I began conducting Google searches on each suspect once I learned their names. I found arrest records and news articles.

I would search for hours, the heat traveling through my body as I felt more and more anger. *Pieces of shit*, I kept thinking. Two of the suspects had been arrested just a few months before Robby's shooting, and yet they were back out on the streets, free to wreak havoc on people's lives. On our lives.

"Carrying a concealed, loaded firearm. Firearm was reported stolen," read a report on one of the suspects, just nine months before Robby's death. Another article on a different suspect read: "Contacted for suspicion of being intoxicated. Found to be in possession of illegal narcotics and a Glock handgun magazine containing 10 rounds of .40 caliber ammunition." And yet how easy it was for them to get their hands on guns again after being released from jail. Guns that killed my son and that were still missing—out in the world, where they could be used to injure or kill others. It was incomprehensible to me.

"Are you still against taking medication?" Marsha asked. "Because you are falling deeper into depression and you still have a trial to think about." I listened to her, not really caring one way or the other. "Imagine a wound, and having that wound re-injured over and over. That is what the trial is going to do to you. You need something that can help you through that. You said you've stopped exercising. Exercising can help balance those emotions. But if you're not going to exercise, I really think you should consider medication."

I went to the gym the next day, running on the elliptical trainer as if my life depended on it—which I guess it did. I went again the next day, and the next, until I slowly built up a regular routine again. During my next therapy session, I let Marsha know of my progress, anticipating the "And how do you feel about that" question. "It gives me an outlet to let my rage out. But I'm still dealing with my anger," I said. "Robby was on his way to something. He was doing something with his life. These people who took his life weren't doing anything meaningful with their lives. It's not fair. It makes me wonder what's the point."

Marsha shifted her chair so that we were now sitting face to face. She looked at me and held my gaze. "Life is not fair or unfair. It is not kind or unkind. It just *is*." I tried to digest and decode her statement, before she began again. "Just because you are feeling angry now does not mean everything you have learned and all the progress you've made this past year are gone. Grief is not linear. PTSD is not linear. You can go from grief to hope to anxiety to hope again. You have been angry at God, but you never allowed yourself to feel angry about the people who did this. You have every right to feel angry. It is natural. Let yourself feel it and experience it."

PSYCHOTHERAPY NOTE

  OBJECTIVE:

  *Updated Mental Status Examination: Mental status normal with exception of following:

  Mood: depressed

  *Updated Risk Assessment:

  Suicide: passive thoughts of death; denies intent plan or means

  Homicide: denies

  *Updated Clinical Status/Relevant History/Active Abuse-Trauma Concerns/Treatment Response:

  Pati returns to therapy after almost a year since son was killed. She reports recently the persons involved have been arrested and there will be a trial. This has re triggered ptsd, thoughts of the shooting, as well and much anger. Pt reports in the interim she has been working 3 jobs to keep busy, but put on weight, been smoking 3–4 cigarettes daily, and not taking care of herself. She reports she has gained 15 pounds. She and other family members wish to leave Solano County and far from Vallejo, but the case is still pending trial. She also reports she has been uncomfortable seeking treatment in Vallejo but does not wish to change to another Clinic. Mood depressed, withdrawn and anxious and fearful that other members of her family may be targeted. She continues to decline pharmacotherapy, but has started going to the gym again and is willing to explore ways to counter depression and anger. Session explores treatment plan.

A week later, on Halloween, I turned on the news and watched the top story about a man named Noah Harpham, 33, who shot three people dead in Colorado Springs before police killed him in a shootout. He had a history of drug and alcohol abuse. A month after that, I turned on the TV and saw a story about a man named Syed Rizwan Farook. He left a Christmas party held at Inland Regional Center in San Bernardino, California and later returned with another person, Tashfeen Malik. The two opened fire, killing 14 and wounding 21. The two were later killed by police as they fled in an SUV.

I imagined the shooters in these stories being raised in troubled homes, their hearts filled with pain and anger. Or perhaps they had been irrevocably damaged by society, bullied and ridiculed by peers growing up, and were now seeking vengeance in a world that rarely showed them kindness. It was no excuse, but it was my only way to understand how we as humans can reach such depths of despair, to the point where taking another person's life was not only possible, but desired. Perhaps it is easier to end another's life when you see no value in your own.

We are all responsible. How we raise our children, how we interact with one another—the effects of those relationships are carried out and perpetuated into the world. Had the suspects in Robby's case been shown more compassion and opportunity in life, where would they be today? I wondered if they would still be sitting in jail cells facing first-degree-murder charges, awaiting their trial, facing 50 years to life in prison. And where would my son be today if they had only chosen to follow a different path?

I told myself the suspects were pieces of shit because it made it easier for me to hate them. By dehumanizing them, I could avoid seeing their worth. But isn't that what they did to Robby? Had they taken a moment to see him as a human being, with a life, a family—had they shown him compassion—would they have been so quick to end his life? This was the unanswerable question that easily took me down a slippery slope, from the safe peak of denial to the murky pit of utter frustration. It was here that I would ask repeatedly: Why, why, why? But I would never get an answer—and even if I did, it would never ease the pain.

I screamed, swore and sat as my blood coursed wildly through my veins, wanting these suspects to pay for what they did. And in the end, the only person I was hurting was myself. Despite my instinct to lash out like a wounded, cornered animal, I had to mentally and emotionally fight to find a shred of compassion, if only for self-preservation. This was not an easy task, and it required hours of introspection. Hours of sitting silently in a chair, alone in our spare room with the door shut. Hours of sitting by Robby's grave, staring at his name above the dates of his birth and death. Hours in my car driving along empty stretches of rural roads, talking myself down from an emotional ledge. Until I had somehow come to terms with what I needed to do.

I had to see them as human beings and not as merely suspects and killers. I had to tell myself they were sons and brothers. And nephews. They were products of lives and relationships I knew nothing about. They were born as we all are, with innocence, not hate. They were human. This could be the starting point to ease the burden of hate I was now carrying. We create the world we live in by the way we treat each other and the way we react to that treatment, good or bad. I didn't understand it then, but I did now.

Life is not fair or unfair. It is not kind or unkind. It just *is*.

Meaning

Chapter 23

Scarecrow

Staff sizes and resources had been steadily dwindling at daily newspapers since the rise of the Internet and the advent of the 24-hour news cycle. Smaller dailies, such as the Vallejo paper, were no exception. In an effort to cut back, the newspaper ended its Monday edition, thus eliminating the need for a full-time Sunday reporter. So on this particular Sunday, longtime staff photographer Mike Jory found himself in uncharted territory, working his first weekend alone as both photographer and reporter. Despite his 30-plus years at the paper, this was a first for him—and he had seen a lot. He was hoping for a slow news day on this inaugural shift, and it looked like it would be, until he heard the call over the police scanner. Someone had been shot. Mike grabbed his camera and notebook and headed to the location. When he arrived, an officer offered him a closer view of the crime scene, but for some reason he declined, taking his photos from afar.

He returned with the basics for his first report: A young man had been killed near a new truck that was his. A spokesman for the police department told him the people who shot him assaulted another man as they left the scene, and that they fled from the incident and hopped onto the freeway. He worked the details into his crime story and proceeded to work on his photos, as he had done hundreds of times before this day. He didn't have the victim's identification because police had yet to contact the next of kin.

The following day, Mike received a call at his home from the newspaper's executive editor, Jack Bungart, who had been working in the sports department during my time at the newspaper. Under other circumstances, the call would not have been made. The police issued their official notice with the victim's name, but Jack didn't need to call Mike. There were other reporters now who could write the follow-up story. This was different. The victim was someone they had both known. It was Robby.

After hearing this, Mike sat silent on the other end of the line, unable to say anything for minutes. He went numb. When he was able to speak, all he could say was one word: "Shit." And then he cried. Even during the city's year of record-number homicides, he had never covered a story where someone he knew had even been injured, let alone died. He thought about how the police had offered him a closer view of the scene, and he was thankful now that he declined. He worried that something in his photo may have caused me and my family more pain. And it was then that he made a commitment to himself to be more understanding. His job would be the same—he would continue taking pictures and sometimes taking on the job of a reporter. Nothing about his job description would change, and yet his approach to it was now changed forever.

Many days I would bring Robby and Julie with me into the newsroom, where Mike first met them as young children. They would go from desk to desk, saying hello, and playing hide-and-seek behind file cabinets. I left the newspaper in 1997, and on my last day I went from one person to the next, bidding my individual farewells and offering well-wishes. I saved Mike for last. "I think you are my scarecrow," I said to him, referencing *The Wizard of Oz*, "because I will miss you most of all." But he was always around for the milestones.

As the children grew older, we would often run into Mike as he covered various stories for the newspaper. He was there at Robby's high school graduation, then at Julie's two years later, taking photos for the front page. He was there for most of Julie's high school volleyball games, capturing great action shots, which we'd clip from the paper the next day. And in the end, he was there when Robby died.

The incident affected him so deeply he took to Facebook to express his emotions:

> *September 23, 2014*
>
> *Working in journalism, you get used to many things happening. This weekend, I reported on an event that at the time, I never realized the personal repercussions it would have.*
>
> *The young man whose shooting death I covered on Sunday has turned out to be the son of a friend and former co-worker. I remember him first as a little boy, playing among the desks in the newsroom. Later, as a much taller than me young man at his sister's graduation. Now, I have a final memory that I wish to God I would never have to have. My sympathies are to his family.*
>
> *Remember, every victim of violence has a family, and they will suffer the pain more than we can realize.*

The post attracted a long list of comments, including this from one of his many friends:

Sounds really hard to witness the entire arc of a child's life. Sorry to hear, Mike. I'm sure it meant a lot to the family that you were there to cover the story.

In fact, I never knew Mike was at the scene at all. He was gone before we arrived, and because I didn't look at the articles, I never saw his name under the photos. It wasn't until I saw his post on Facebook that I realized he was sent to cover the story. He became a close family friend, making his way through the crowd at the funeral to give me a long, tight embrace.

"Remember when you said I was the scarecrow?" he asked me, his eyes filled with tears. And at that moment I really pictured myself as Dorothy, and he the Scarecrow, both of us wishing for something and someplace that made us feel whole.

It wasn't until two years later that I found the courage to ask Mike the details of that day. It never occurred to me that his life had also changed because of it. He said he had seen enough shootings and death in his career, and without it being someone personal, someone can become inured to the action. But since then, he had recovered much of his empathy for anyone involved in a crime scene. *Even when it's someone who was in the wrong. They all have family. They all have been loved. They all are equally dead.*

Robby's death "pulled the scab off," he messaged me, and unlike before, he couldn't approach a crime scene the same way anymore. He couldn't see a victim without thinking of that person's life or the family they left behind. *I spend much more time considering every aspect of the photo shot and worrying about details that could cause pain.* And even after his decades as a journalist, he suddenly realized the injustice of our collective complacency when it came to the growing number of shootings in the news. We should care more, even if we don't know who they are. And our concern should last longer than the time it takes to disappear from the news cycle.

It was a revelation to me—that Robby's death had changed the course of other people's lives beyond our own small circle. That people directly or indirectly involved in his life and death were affected, and because of that, they had changed their perspectives on life and the decisions they made. It was all part of the ripple effect, both good and bad. It was pain transformed into something positive. One newspaper photographer who now approached his job with more empathy, more compassion, more understanding. And that had the potential to affect hundreds of people whose loved ones were taken by tragedy and whose crime scenes would be photographed.

"I have learned something from Robby," Mike said. "And it's a lesson I would gladly have passed up on having reason to learn."

Chapter 24

Robby's Shop

We pulled into the large parking lot, scanning the various buildings in search of the main entrance. "Where are you guys now?" Ruben texted.

"We just entered the lot, I can see a flagpole," I replied.

"Drive toward the flagpole. I'll wait for you there."

Cicero maneuvered the car toward the meeting spot, where we found Ruben waving us down and pointing to a vacant parking space. It was there that I also spotted others getting out of their cars, walking toward the building—my brother and sister-in-law; cousins, friends, my mom, Ruben's family.

Mike was among the first people who arrived. When Ruben told me that Genentech, the biotech company where Robby had been working before he died, wanted to hold a ceremony dedicating its weld shop to Robby, I wanted Mike there. He was going to take photographs for the newspaper, showing that Robby's life meant something. In the short time he worked at the company, he made enough of an impact that they were now dedicating a part of the building to him. But there were too many legal issues involved with that since Genentech was a large, international company. The request to have media there would have to go through a lengthy vetting process through the company's legal team for approval. "I still want you to come," I messaged Mike. "You are part of the family."

Mostly, I wanted to help erase his last memory of Robby from his mind and replace it with something positive. I spotted him already signing in at the reception desk, his ever-present camera hanging from his neck. "Thanks for coming," I told him, giving him a big hug. "Wouldn't miss it," he said.

There were about 20 of us gathered in the lobby by the time we were escorted through the building and into the department where Robby worked. We rounded the corner from an office space filled with cubicles into a large, open space with a high ceiling. Long tables were set out with various bowls and platters filled with all kinds of food—smoked Hawaiian kalua pork, noodle dishes, stews, lasagna, barbecue, salads, breads, rice, sweets. Chairs were set up along rows of covered tables, as approximately 50-plus employees stood against the walls.

"Everyone did this. Everyone contributed food and put this together. They wanted to do it for Robby," said Craig Doerfert, who headed the department Robby worked in. He was also Ruben's boss. I looked around at the space, the tools and equipment that Robby had told me so much about. I looked at the people, his co-workers, some clearly overcome with emotion themselves as they approached me, Julie and the rest of our family.

He was a great guy to work with.

He was so talented.

Such a hard worker.

Craig led us past the tables and through an entryway to the weld shop where Robby had spent hours on this newly found passion. He would bring in his speakers and blast songs reflecting his eclectic taste in music. "Mostly alternative island reggae," said one of his co-workers. "He used to play it really loud while he was welding.

You could just tell he was having fun." We could hear the music getting louder as we walked closer to the shop. They had Robby's playlist on, turned up to his preferred volume: loud.

And then we were there. Right above the shop was a huge customized sign made of stainless steel that read *Robby's Shop*, with an image of a welder on each side. To the right of the door was a framed photo of Robby, the same image we brought with us to Hawaii, with his arms folded and a large grin on his face. It was overwhelming. He was not even a full-time employee, and yet he now had a part of the building permanently dedicated to him. I felt enormous pride and humility.

"Please, come here any time you want to be in his shop," said Craig. "Any time at all."

We were asked to return to our chairs so Craig could start the dedication ceremony with a speech. He was a young executive, stylishly dressed in his tailored suit. He had an air of authority to him, and I could see that he was deeply respected. Perhaps it was because of this that the many employees who now stood around us looked shocked and deeply moved when Craig struggled to deliver his speech. His voice cracked as he fought through his tears. "I'm sorry," he kept saying, as if he, too, was surprised by his emotion.

Today, we are dedicating the weld shop located at the Vacaville Facilities Building 4 maintenance shop to Robby Poblete. Thank you all for participating in our celebration of Robby Poblete's life and our dedication of one of his favorite and inspirational places to work. I would like to acknowledge and thank Robby's family and friends who are here to celebrate with our Facilities family.

In the short time Robby worked in Maintenance Operations, he made a significant impact on many of our lives. His passing made us look deeper into our current relationships. It made us appreciate what we were able to get from Robby and were able to give Robby. In the past few months, we have heard and shared so many stories about Robby that highlight his passion and thirst for knowledge, experience and building relationships. His passion for cooking, a drink concoction that I think Ruben is still trying to figure out what was in it, his cycling adventures and impressive rides from Suisun to Sacramento, a lot of reading on different topics and so much more. The stories behind these passions are the stories that will keep Robby alive in all our hearts.

 I want to thank many of you for what you gave Robby. He came to Maintenance Operations as a young man with a desire to learn more about his father's trade. This was a wonderful relationship to observe: a father teaching his son and both building another level of closeness in their relationship. Many of you participated in this relationship and the development of Robby, and I thank you for what you gave; the Poblete family I am sure offer the same thanks. Dana, Ruel, Ruben, you were the trio that really introduced Robby to the welding world and the metalworking trade, and it stuck. Robby spent many of his hours in the welding shop supporting the many projects that came through Facilities. I love the story Ruben shared with me where one day, he just looked through the weld window, looking at his son, so proud of him and so happy he found another passion he would pursue. In fact, Robby was so inspired he began purchasing all of the metalworking equipment to build a similar weld

*shop in his father's garage. Ruben is going to finish this
dream for Robby.*

*It is with great honor and gratitude that we dedi-
cate this weld shop to a member of our family who is
gone too soon, but will always be remembered: Robby
Poblete.*

When Craig's speech ended, they turned Robby's music back on,
people lined up to stack their plates with food, and various groups
began posing under the "Robby's Shop" sign for pictures. I imagined the men and women who worked there, present and future,
some remembering Robby—others, years from now, staring at the
framed picture, wondering who he was and what kind of life he
led. They might wonder what he did to deserve the plaque and the
sign with his name that hung so largely over the shop they now
worked in. But I would know.

Despite the brevity of his time in the company and on Earth, he
had inspired others with his passion for life. For a brief moment
in time, this was where he worked, repairing and creating with his
hands as his music choreographed his moves and echoed through
the building—letting everyone around him know: Robby was here,
and he *lived*.

Chapter 25

All In

The Vallejo Yacht Club sat tucked away along the city's waterfront. Flowing between the clubhouse and Mare Island was the Mare Island Strait, an extension of the Napa River. Founded in 1900, it was the fifth oldest yacht club in the San Francisco Bay Area. And despite its now-craggy exterior, the club's members were among the area's elite, socially and economically. Among the highlights of its long history were a club visit by Clark Gable and membership by Jack London. The club's mission: "To encourage yachting, rowing and aquatic sports; to promote good fellowship and the social interest and pleasure of the members of this corporation."

Robby didn't know any of this. He just wanted to buy a sailboat. Somewhere between his passion for this and his obsession with that, Robby took an interest in sailing. And as with all his interests, he went all in. He knocked on the front door of the Yacht Club one day, with no appointment or connections, and explained that he was interested in sailing. He didn't have money to become a member, but he knew how to cook. So they took him in, most of them older men who took a liking to this curious kid who randomly showed up at the doorstep of their historical clubhouse. They took him on sailing trips around the San Francisco Bay and invited him to special events and sailing races along the waterfront. He showed off his cooking skills, taking advantage of their full kitchen, and he made many friends, despite the fact that most of the members had two decades on him.

"What do old white men drink?" Robby asked Cicero and me one day. He came out of his room, dressed for a social event at the club. Members would take turns providing alcohol, and it was Robby's turn. He was wearing high-waisted khakis, a tucked-in polo short and a canvas belt with a metal buckle in the shape of a sailboat. He looked like he was in his 60s.

"Are you trying to dress like them?" I asked. Cicero let out a laugh.

"What?" Robby responded, looking at himself in the mirror. "So what do they like to drink?"

"Budweiser," we both responded.

A few hours later, he returned, his face flushed. "Old white men can drink," he mumbled, before falling into a long, deep sleep on the couch.

His time as an honorary member took up most of his weekends and afternoons. After returning from daylong sailing trips, he'd often come home exhausted and inspired. "I want to live on a boat one day," he announced. "I want to be able to sail wherever I want and be near the water."

One of the club's younger members was soon returning to his home in Alaska and encouraged Robby to come with him. "My friend said there's lots of jobs there on the boats." But Ruben and I were reluctant. Alaska seemed like a world away, and the only thing he'd be bringing with him was the promise of a job.

"If you can save enough money to go," I said, as a compromise.

Ruben was against the idea, even if he did raise the money. "What if he ends up finding someone and he never moves back?" he asked me one day.

It was a moot point. Robby's friend needed an answer within weeks, and Robby wasn't prepared to go. By that time, the Yacht Club began asking him to pay membership dues, and Robby took that as his cue to go. He retained everything he had learned from them, hoping the knowledge would come in handy when he saved enough money. "I'll become a member when I buy my boat," he said, confident he would return.

～

"Check this out, Mom."

I knew what that meant. It was what he said every time he'd buy something new, learn a new trick or discover a new interest. It was a statement that indicated for the next few months—maybe even a year—he would be engaged in a self-imposed, full immersion: reading, practicing, experimenting, perfecting the art of whatever it was he was interested in at the time.

I followed him through the sliding door and into the backyard. He walked toward the side of the house where he had turned a bucket upside down and placed an octagon-shaped foam target on top of it. He crouched down and picked up a huge bow, selecting an arrow from a bunch. He pulled the bow back and released, sending the arrow flying through the air and directly into the center of the target. "Wow!" I said, genuinely impressed.

"Now watch this," he said, already grabbing the next arrow. He took his time, closing one eye, focusing his target and slightly moving his position. He pulled back the bow, releasing the arrow once again. I turned my head, following its trail, and watched it stick into the back of the previous arrow. "They call that a Robin Hood," he said.

"How long have you been practicing this?" I asked.

"A while," he answered with a broad grin, clearly surprised and pleased that his gamble paid off. He had been making the shot maybe 30 percent of the time before calling me to come watch him.

He brought his bow and arrows to family parties, often challenging his uncles. Their arms would shake against the tension of the bow as they tried desperately to pull it back, arrows flying dangerously and aimlessly into the sky. Robby would shake his head and cover his mouth in disbelief. "Put that away," I said one day as one of his uncles shot an arrow straight through the fence and into the (luckily) empty sidewalk.

Perhaps one of his longer and more costly obsessions was with fish. He came home one day, his car loaded with three huge fish tanks that he had acquired from a fish store owner he befriended. I imagined him showing up at the store, explaining his love of fish and asking if there was any spare equipment he could take off his hands to pursue his interest.

"Where are these going to go?" I asked in a panic.

"My room," he answered.

Our water bill spiked that first month as he regularly emptied and refilled the tanks, exploring different ways to position and decorate them. He went through numerous fish: a silver arowana, African cichlids, clown knife. At night, we'd hear the endless hum of the filters rising through his ceiling and through our bedroom floor. It was as if we lived above a pet store. He bought numerous books on freshwater fish, learning everything he could before gradually moving on to a new interest. After more than a year, the tanks were emptied and tossed and the fish fondly remembered.

But cooking was his passion. It was a constant that we all benefitted from, save for the fact that my kitchen would be left in complete turmoil: my counters grainy with the residue of scattered spices from around the world; walls and ceiling splattered with colorful sauces; stovetop caked with mystery substances.

His food was always amazing, if not bordering on dangerous levels of heat. He loved to experiment with different flavors, often going to Mediterranean, Thai and Indian markets to buy exotic spices. "Try this, Mom," he'd say, dipping a ladle into one of his big pots, splattering sauce all over the floor as our dogs ran to lick it up. I'd give it a taste, my mouth soon exploding with heat and my face breaking into a sweat. "You think that's spicy?" he'd say.

He made a variety of curries and stews. Inspired by Indian flavors, he began inventing new dishes using eggplant, okra and lentils. He had just begun experimenting with grains, such as quinoa and couscous, before he became distracted by a shiny object called a smoker. One summer he came home with the black, metal cooker, determined to learn the art of smoking meats. He marveled at his first crimson-colored smoke ring as he cut into a beef brisket that had spent hours in the smoker. He researched what type of wood chips to buy, different dry rubs and smoking techniques.

At the time he had been dating a girl named Rachel. Poor, sweet Rachel. I'd watched her through the kitchen window several nights, shivering in the cold with a blanket wrapped around her as Robby fed his smoker with wood chips, checking on the meat until the wee hours of the night. He still hadn't perfected the timing of the whole process. But by 3:00 a.m., they would have a perfectly smoked piece of meat. "Look at that smoke ring!" he'd say to her as she struggled to keep her eyes open.

"Robby, you should have a cooking show," I said, looking around my war-torn kitchen. "And they should call it *The Sloppy Chef*."

The hobbies were not hobbies to him, but stages of his life that he learned from and carried with him. Hobbies implied they were fleeting, whereas he invested time in learning everything he could, he argued. And in that sense he had become an "expert" in table tennis, target shooting, sailing, archery, cooking, smoking meats, Muay Thai, fish tanks and the fish in them, tattooing, swimming, welding, world religions, cycling, surfing, yoga, yoga surfing, yo-yos, meditation, skateboarding—to name a few.

"If you're going to do something, you might as well go all in," he said. "Otherwise, what's the point?"

Chapter 26

Always Forward

The lights had turned off in the cabin of United Airlines Flight 837 bound for Tokyo. I would have a three-hour layover at Narita International Airport before catching a connecting flight to Manila. Luckily, I was in an aisle seat and I could use the time to prepare for my presentation. I turned on my reading light, unlatched my meal tray and placed my laptop on top of it.

For the past year I had kept myself occupied, taking on a new full-time job, while also working as a consultant for two other companies focused on environmental sustainability. People worried that I was drowning myself in work, but ironically, it was the work that kept me afloat. I had been focused on a project with the Philippines Climate Change Commission and the Office of the Presidential Adviser for Environmental Protection. Both were government agencies that reported directly to Philippine President Benigno Aquino III. He was the son of former Philippine President Corazon Aquino and Benigno Aquino Jr., a former senator who was assassinated at Manila International Airport (now Ninoy Aquino International Airport), where I would be landing in approximately 13 hours. Phill would meet me in Manila, where we would then catch the next flight to the country's southern islands of Mindanao.

It was perhaps one of my most arduous journeys, requiring an additional 13-hour drive once we landed, where I would be taken directly to a meeting with leaders of seven indigenous tribes in the region. No time to change, or even wash my face. The big meeting would immediately follow, during which we would meet with various local government agencies and one of President Aquino's key advisers, Secretary Nereus Acosta—or, as I had come to know him, "Neric."

The meeting took place in Bukidnon, Neric's hometown, where his family had established deep political and social roots. His mother had once served as mayor, and his father was Dr. Juan Acosta, a well-known and respected horticulture and plant-breeding scientist in the country. The family owned large amounts of land in Bukidnon, which they used in a variety of ways, mostly for farming and housing.

Among Neric's latest ventures was an eco-adventure park, called Kampo Juan, where he and an engineering team had set up activities such as ziplining, rappelling and a suspension bridge spanning 360 feet across a ravine and 200 feet above a winding river. But its main attraction was the first of its kind in the country—a suspended bike ride called the "Anicycle" that involved riding a bicycle on a cable that hung 100 feet over a ravine, with an expanse the length of 600 feet. So daring were the activities that Kampo Juan was chosen as a site for *The Amazing Race Philippines*. In addition, the park included more than six acres of plant breeding and a demo farm where organic crops were cultivated by Dr. Acosta himself. It attracted students and farmers who were interested in innovative, organic and sustainable agricultural practices from across the country.

"Why don't you be my guest at Kampo Juan while you are here?" said Neric. As the president's key adviser on environmental issues, he was based in Manila, but he made a special trip for our meeting. I suspected it had to do with Robby. I hadn't seen Neric since Robby died, and the only communication we'd had was a beautiful handwritten card he sent me expressing his condolences. It was more than I ever expected from a high-ranking official whom I had only come to know through work. But like Katsu, and like Phill, he had become a close friend. "You and Phill, please visit our humble place."

It didn't take much to convince us. I was exhausted, but I needed a break from presentations and meetings. Neric arranged for us to stay at an exclusive lodge surrounded by sweeping pineapple fields. Bordering the plantation was the natural grandeur of the Kitanglad Mountain Ranges, which was classified as a protected area thanks to legislation authored by Neric.

"Welcome!" He beckoned to Phill and me, arms wide open. It reminded me of Ricardo Montalbán in *Fantasy Island*. He stopped in front of me, placed his hands on my shoulders and looked directly at me. "How are you coping?" he asked.

It was a question that made me want to cry. "How are you?" was the question I was frequently asked—by the cashier at the grocery store, the bank teller, neighbors getting their mail. It was also asked by my close friends and relatives, and as always, I'd answer "Fine, and you?" Because no one really asks the question expecting to hear the truth. It's a phrase that has become a mere greeting. *How are you coping* implied a deeper concern. It acknowledged a struggle. And it recognized a need to deal with that struggle.

"I'm stronger now," I replied for the first time. A response I never gave when asked how I was.

"Well, don't worry about anything while you are here. You are my guest. Just take everything in and enjoy yourself."

We climbed into his large truck as he instructed his driver to take us to Kampo Juan. Bukidnon was the home of Del Monte's pineapple plantation and had been since 1926. The region's rich, red soil, high elevation and cooler climes made it ideal for the crop. We passed numerous farms, plantations and buildings, each one soliciting a historical narrative from Neric, including the very spot where General Douglas MacArthur and his party had come to the Del Monte Airfield before he famously declared, "I shall return."

We bounced around in the truck as it cut through overgrown vegetation along a narrow dirt trail. Neric pointed out the different crops his father was growing before the truck came to a stop in front of a large wooden structure that resembled a huge treehouse. It was then that Neric transformed from a politician into a young child, excited to show us his new toys. "Come, follow me!" he said. I watched him as he took us through the various guest rooms, pointing out how the structure was built to fit in with nature—tree trunks in the middle of rooms, showers surrounded by treetops and shrubs, water filtering through bamboo. It was unlike anything I had ever seen.

"Robby would have loved this!" I said.

"He's here," said Neric. "He is everywhere you are."

We then followed him to the "adventure" part of the eco-adventure park, though Phill made it clear he would not be participating due to an "incident" he suffered during the park's early, experimental days. "No way. I'll just stay here and take pictures," he said, as I signed the various legal waivers.

First was the zipline, higher and longer than any zipline I had ever seen anywhere else. The only other time I had ziplined was when we went to Hawaii for Robby's one-year anniversary. Julie wanted us all to go, and so we did, unclear of what it would entail. And though it was both frightening and exhilarating, it was a pony ride compared with this. I stood on top of the first platform looking down to . . . nothing. All I could see below me were dots of treetops and what looked like a piece of string.

"That's the river!" said Neric. My palms began to sweat.

"I'll go first!" he said, barely containing his excitement. He lifted his legs and lunged himself forward, hanging upside down, then right-side up with his arms in the air. It seemed like forever until he reached the other end.

"Your turn, ma'am," said one of the park's employees, standing on the platform next to me.

Holy shit, I thought. *No freakin' way.*

"C'mon, Pati!" yelled Neric from across the way, his voice echoing through all the open space between us.

"Don't be scared, ma'am. Just relax," said the worker. I felt like I was going to faint. My heart was racing and my sweaty palms could barely grip my harness "Don't be scared," he said again.

I took a deep breath, lifted my legs, sat back and flew forward, along the cable and above the wooded area beneath me. I could hear Neric's voice beckoning, "You did it!" I kept my eyes focused on the platform ahead, where he stood to the side, cheering me on. The brakes would kick in, and I would have to plant my feet on the ground for a smooth landing. It was all I could focus on for now.

"Amazing!" Neric said, when I made it over. "Now the bridge!"

We hiked to the suspension bridge, which looked like nothing more than a leap of faith held together by twine. Neric had a wicked look on his face, and I knew he was planning to jump and rattle the bridge as I walked across. "If you so much as sneeze I'm going to turn around and leave," I said, with a serious, threatening tone.

"Well, that's no fun," he responded, walking along the bridge with ease as my hands trembled with each, overly thought-out step. When I finally made it to the other side, Neric stood with two workers waiting to strap me into the last, most challenging activity—the Anicycle.

I stood on a wooden board staring at the two cables in front of me. On each cable was a bicycle, its rubber tires replaced with metal wheels, grooved in the middle to allow the bike to sit flatly on the cable. Two other cables attached the bike to a cable above, where the rider's harness would also be attached. "No matter what, don't pedal backward," the worker warned me as he strapped me in with all the cables.

"What happens when you pedal backward?" I asked, my voice trembling.

"Just don't," he said. "Always forward, always forward!"

Neric was already strapped into the bicycle on the cable next to me, pedaling before they even gave him the signal. "Let's go!" he yelled, looking back at me. I was frozen. I didn't want to move. Now all I could think of was pedaling backward. I didn't know what would happen because he wouldn't tell me, but I knew it wasn't good. Neric kept looking back, waiting for me to catch up.

"I don't want to!" I snapped.

"You can do it!" he yelled. He stretched out his arm toward me. "Take my hand," he said, with a look of comfort. "Just take my hand."

I inhaled through my nose, exhaled through my mouth. I thought of Robby and all of his interests and passions. His fearlessness and thirst for adventure. His willingness to try anything and everything, and approach anyone as a means of expanding his view of life. I used this to fuel my courage as I began to pedal.

"Remember, always forward!" yelled the worker behind me.

"It's okay," I told Neric when I reached him. "I don't need to take your hand. I can do it.

"If I'm going to do something, I might as well go all in."

I was pedaling in mid-air, the closest to biking with Robby in the heavens as I could come. I felt alive, my fear, anxiety and anger left on the platform behind me. My spirit untethered, embracing the blue sky and green canvas below. Moving forward.

Always forward.

Joy

Chapter 27

The Strong One

One month after Facebook COO Sheryl Sandberg's husband died, she opened up about her tragic loss through a post on her Facebook page on June 3, 2015. She described the Jewish tradition of shiva, a seven-day period of intense mourning after the loved one is buried. While life resumed afterward, it was the end of sheloshim, 30 days after burial, that marked the completion of religious mourning. The ritualistic themes resonated with me, having gone through the nine-day novena, then the 40th day that marked Robby's ascension into heaven in the Catholic faith. The parallels intrigued me enough to read her entire post. One statement in particular touched me deeply, and it was a sentiment that I had thought of repeatedly since Robby's death:

When people say to me, "You and your children will find happiness again," my heart tells me, Yes, I believe that, but I know I will never feel pure joy again.

Pure joy. Before the tragedy, I knew what that felt like. It was the feeling I had when I gave birth to both my children, hearing them cry for the first time and knowing what every new parent knows: That from that day on, I would love them more than I would love myself. It was the feeling I had when I'd see my newborns yawn. I'd rush to inhale, taking in the sweet smell of their breath. It was watching them take their first steps, then before I knew it, watching them walk the line at graduation, holding up their diplomas over their heads. It was what I felt watching them open Christmas gifts and seeing them in their first relationships. It was a feeling that came with an open, hopeful heart—a feeling that at that moment, everyone was safe, happy and whole. Everything was *good*.

But now just a glimmer of joy came with other things. Guilt and sadness. Mostly sadness. *I wish he were here* is the thought that quickly entered my mind every time I experienced a hint of happiness. I doubted I could ever feel pure joy again, because that would mean letting go of that thought. Sweetness would always be coupled with the bitterness of one, inescapable reality: *He is not here.*

It was an emotional tightrope that I was learning how to balance: happiness, guilt and sadness, all intertwined to form a new, unfamiliar and tortured emotion. There were times when I would find myself laughing at something or humming a tune, and I would feel immense guilt. I'd stop and force myself to think about the crime scene, the funeral, everything, just to bring myself back to a crippling state of grief. One that I thought I should constantly be in. I didn't know how to allow myself to be happy, to feel pure joy, without a part of me saying that it was wrong.

A few weeks after I read Sandberg's post, Julie was set to graduate from her program at the Fashion Institute of Design & Merchandising. It had been a grueling year for her, having resumed the program only one month after her brother's death. She suffered anxiety and numerous panic attacks during classes, but still managed to push through.

"She deserves a party," I told both Ruben and Cicero. It would be the first big gathering at our house since the nine days of prayer the previous year. And it would be the first time many people would be seeing us again since the funeral.

In the spirit of Robby's mantra, I went all in, hiring various caterers to put together a diverse buffet of Asian and Polynesian foods. Two servers were stationed at a booth in the garage, poised to assemble fusion tacos and various flavors of shave ice on demand. I ordered a huge banner with her photo that read *Congratulations, Julie!*, which spanned the length of the wall where it hung. We set up more tables in the backyard where I had converted my potting bench into a full bar. I ordered shot glasses as party favors with a logo of Julie's name, the year and a graduation cap.

More than 200 people RSVP'd after invitations went out, and for weeks leading up to the party I wondered whether I had gone too far. It was too late now. I found every open space in our house, the backyard, the front yard and even the sides of the house and set up as many tables and chairs as I could. I hired a DJ without even knowing where he would go. "This is a good spot," he said. He came over a day before the party to see what space he was dealing with. I hadn't thought of the equipment he'd bring or the space he'd need to set it all up. He was standing now in a nook by our dining table between the kitchen and the family room. It was the spot where we had set up the altar with Robby's pictures during the prayers.

"That's fine," I said, feeling the guilt course through me. I hired a photographer to capture candid moments, and I arranged for my sister-in-law and Julie's godfather to serve as bartenders, a job they gladly accepted.

It was early morning the day of the party and I had a full list of things to do before guests would start arriving at 2:00 p.m. I still had to pick up food, set up decorations, arrange more tables and chairs and clear the space for the DJ. I crawled out of bed and walked to Robby's room. I sat on his meditation cushion facing the window that looked out into the hills. I wasn't meditating so much as I was communicating with him. *Today is your sister's graduation party*, I told him in silence. *I wish you were here to celebrate with us. But I know you will be, in some way. I hope you are proud of her. She did this for you.*

And then I made a declaration, which was really my way of asking for permission. From him. From the universe. From myself.

I will celebrate without feeling sadness, without feeling guilt. I will feel joy for my daughter and I will send love to my son. Because they both deserve it. And I deserve it.

By 1:00 p.m., I had merged our long dining table with the built-in island in the kitchen, forming one long buffet table. All the chafing dishes had been labeled and separated into different stations, depending on what country the food represented. Cookies and customized cupcakes with Julie's name on them were placed on different tiers, forming a tower of sweets. Condiments, napkins and party favors were placed on each setting at every table. The DJ had already set up multicolor lights swirling around the family room and Earth, Wind & Fire was playing softly in the background to greet guests.

By 3:00 p.m., the house was packed, with every table filled. A line had formed at the taco and shave-ice station. The backyard bar had become a hot spot. And a constant, steady line moved around the buffet table. The music was loud now, alternating from salsa to R&B to island reggae, which I requested for Robby. Julie was approached by guests, all offering their congratulations and expressing how proud they were of her.

Before sunset, I looked through the crowds for Ruben and Cicero. Ruben was in the front, surrounded by people from Genentech. I found Cicero in the backyard speaking to friends I had known since middle school. "Let's gather everyone," I said. I asked the DJ for a microphone and to stop the music. We called the guests to the backyard. Julie sat on a bar stool, facing everyone. I stood with the mic, flanked by both Cicero and Ruben, each of us holding a fresh floral lei. I asked my brother, Chris, to give a little speech since Ruben, Cicero and I were too emotional to speak. I looked around at all the people, more than I thought our backyard could ever hold. We were surrounded by the garden I had spent countless hours in, planting, crying, smiling, healing. I felt like my plants were among the guests who deserved to be part of the celebration.

"We want to thank you all for coming and celebrating this day with us," Chris started. "It really means a lot to all of us. It's been a really hard year for our family, and we want to thank you all for the support you've shown us." My eyes went from one familiar face to the next, before landing on Julie. "We are so proud of you and what you've been able to accomplish, despite everything. Your brother would be so proud of you. We know you'll accomplish great things." I heard sniffles coming from different directions now, as people began to cry.

"To Julie!" he said abruptly, raising his glass, avoiding his own waterworks.

The guests toasted and cheered, wiping their eyes as each of us, Ruben, Cicero and I, stepped forward to place our leis around Julie's neck. People looked on, their expressions saying it all. They were happy that we were all okay, and that despite everything, we were here together for something positive.

"It's good to see you," one of my former colleagues said as she and her family prepared to leave. She squeezed my arm and took her time for emphasis, "No, it's *really* good to see you." I knew what she meant. The last time most of these guests were in our home, I could barely make eye contact with anyone. My eyes were red and swollen, my face ashen, my mouth dry from dehydration. Our home was filled with shock and grief, and the despair was palpable. People entered and exited in sorrow, not knowing what would become of us. But somehow we found our way, and we continued to.

The DJ was playing salsa music now. A few of my girlfriends came in from the backyard and began to dance. I heard Ruben in the front, laughing as he shared funny stories about Robby working in the weld shop. Cicero was standing by the desserts, intoxicated by the possibilities. Robby's friends were gathered in his room upstairs, sitting on and around the furniture he built with his own hands. They were smiling, eating, looking through his books and various trinkets. I looked over at Julie, surrounded by her friends, laughing, dancing and posing for pictures. The party continued past midnight—and even longer for those who couldn't drive home and ended up sleeping over. It had been a long time since our home was filled with such scenes.

He should be here.

It was a longing that I had come to accept. A void that would never be filled. But in the absence of pure joy, I was grateful for moments of happiness.

Chapter 28

Love and Basketball

My ears were ringing as the crowd of 20,000-plus fans was chanting, stomping and roaring. Everyone was on their feet at Oracle Arena in Oakland, all eyes focused on the team that had brought excitement back to the Golden State Warriors franchise. We were seated in the lower level—seats that were neither easy nor cheap to obtain as the team's popularity soared. But I had insisted. The Warriors were on a streak and had stunned NBA fans across the country as they steamrolled over teams with players much larger and more seasoned than their own.

"Here, just watch this," Cicero, a longtime Warriors fan, said to me that first year. "The Warriors have been playing really well." It was the safest option he could think of.

I had given up on watching television. Even seemingly harmless programs would startle me with an unexpected gun scene. Sometimes the plot would suddenly take a turn, focusing on themes such as death—or even worse, relationships between parents and their children. A wedding, a graduation, a birthday scene. Anything that dealt with issues of the human condition would leave me in emotional shambles. If I was lucky, I'd be able to escape a show without having to endure themes of loss or love, but then the commercials were always risky, especially for movies. I never noticed before how prominent guns were in movie trailers—shooting, aiming, carrying. They'd show up on the screen and I'd instinctively turn my head and plug my ears with my fingers, because I knew the sound of gunshots would likely follow.

So we tried basketball, where commercials mainly consisted of shoes, cars, energy drinks, athletic gear and nutritional supplements. It started out as a means of distraction, progressing to a casual-fan phase and finally into a full-blown passion. I had an emotional investment in each player, bemoaning their losses and celebrating their wins as if my own son were on the team. There were days during that first year when I couldn't get out of bed. But if I knew it was game day, there was something to look forward to. I'd schedule my whole day around game time, making sure I'd cook in time to be seated in front of the television to catch the pre-game commentaries and interviews. I had something to root for, and that kind of positive energy played a big part in pulling me out of depression.

I looked at the ticket prices on my computer screen. I didn't want to sit in the nosebleeds. I wanted to see the players. I wanted to be part of the action near the floor. Before I knew it, I was punching in my credit card number for three seats: Cicero, Julie and me.

"We're going to the game," I told him, placing the printout of the tickets on his desk. He just looked at me. I had refused attending parties and being anywhere with large crowds, except when I was on business trips overseas. But now I wanted to go to Oracle—a venue so loud and boisterous that it had earned the name "Roaracle." My excitement for the team overcame my fear of the crowd, and he wasn't about to question it.

The woman seated in the row in front of us was attracting a lot of attention. People were approaching her, asking to take pictures with her. A cameraman was seated diagonally to her, filming. "Who is that?" I asked Julie, leaning over.

Julie turned her head to look. "No idea," she responded.

The game began in regular fashion for the Warriors, with a pre-game introduction of each of the starting players. The arena went pitch black. Over the 360-degree Jumbotron hanging from the center of the arena, a montage played of city landmarks interspersed with action shots of the players. At the end, dancers carrying large Warriors flags came out running circles around the Warriors logo at the center of the floor. The players were called out one by one, the crowd cheering louder with every name. Flashing lights, pyrotechnics and utter madness ensued. And I was part of it, yelling as loudly as I could.

The lady in front of us began yelling "Day-Day!," a nickname given to one of the star players, Draymond Green, by his mother. And then I realized she was his mom, Mary Babers-Green. After the first quarter, Julie and I made our way over to her, now asking to take a picture with her ourselves. We had a brief conversation, after which I returned to my seat and followed her on Twitter, where she had become famous for her outspoken tweets.

The team won by the end of the night and went on to continue their streak of victories. I was surprised by the emotional connection I felt to them, but it had become clear to me that in addition to gardening, this team had become part of my healing process. And for some reason, I felt compelled to let them know. So I sat in front of my laptop after work one day and, without planning to, I began to write a letter:

An Open Letter to the Golden State Warriors
By Pati Navalta Poblete
During your March 1 game against the Atlanta

Hawks, my daughter, fiancé and I were seated in Section 124, seats 12, 13 and 14. A cameraman was seated at the end of the row in front of us, focusing his lens on a smiling, animated woman. We wondered who she was until she yelled out "C'mon, Day-Day!" And we knew it was your mom, Draymond. We waited until the end of the first quarter, making our way over to ask if she wouldn't mind taking a picture with my daughter. Mary Babers-Green could not be more gracious. After telling her I was among her many followers on Twitter, she replied, "Well, let me know who you are. We're family now!"

I wished at that moment that Mary and I were somewhere else, someplace a bit quieter than the Oracle, so I could explain how true that statement really felt to me. Following the success of her son— along with all of yours—during your 2014–2015 season helped me grieve the loss of my own son, in a way that I could never have expected.

On Sept. 21, 2014, my son was killed by gun violence in Vallejo, Ca., in broad daylight at a busy intersection. Just one hour before he was shot, I had texted him to let him know I was making dinner, and he texted me back to let me know he'd be coming home. And then my whole life changed. It's a call that no parent should ever receive, and a pain so consuming and merciless that it is beyond description. I always say that I wouldn't wish that pain on anyone—not even those who chose to take my son's life away. Robby was 23 years old.

The community rallied around our family and

gathered at our home every night for prayers, to bring food, to let us know they were there for us. But when your child is taken in such a tragic way, a room full of people is no different than a room by yourself. There is no consolation, no feeling of "this will pass"—only questions, confusion, pain and emptiness.

There were so many things I could no longer watch on television. I never realized before how much violence there is on TV—and by now I was diagnosed with depression and PTSD. My severe anxiety and panic attacks prevented me from going anywhere with large crowds of people. I was put on psychiatric disability and couldn't work.

And then I started watching your games.

Sacramento Kings on Oct. 29. Lakers, Nov. 1. Blazers. Clippers. Rockets. All wins. And slowly, I started to come back to life. Following two losses afterward, you went on a 16-game winning streak and the buzz surrounding your team grew louder. Sure, it was exciting to watch as a fan, but for me it meant something more. Much has been said about your individual characters, but I don't think it can be overstated how you've not only transformed the game, but transcended it. You have fun out there. You're selfless with the ball. You praise one another during interviews. You don't lift yourselves up by putting other teams or players down. You are all role models in a sport that many believe is fueled by trash-talking and self-aggrandizing.

For me, you represent what I wish for all young men—success through determination, hard work, humility and respect. And you represent what I wish for all mothers—a chance to watch their sons grow into role models. A chance to be proud of who they raised. A chance to watch them live a life worth emulating.

Through your many community programs and volunteer work, you are already changing and improving countless lives. Stopping violence and bullying through your "Not on Our Ground" program. Increasing financial skills in youth through Future Leaders. Impacting lives of underserved youth through your Warriors Community Foundation. These are programs that our youth desperately need, particularly those in communities that are most vulnerable to crime and violence. I have to believe that those who took my son's life would have chosen another path, had they had the guidance and opportunity you are providing.

And so I continue to watch in amazement and pride. I still miss my son every day, and I face his upcoming birthday on April 1 with a deep sadness. He would have been 26, not too far from many of your own ages. But there is something about watching all of you that gives me hope. That as you continue to change the game, you continue to change the way many young boys and men see the world. That you can get ahead while still being kind. That working together leads to success, and that a brotherhood can be forged among strangers.

This is what I wanted to tell Mary. But most of all, this is what I wanted to tell you, Steph, Klay, Draymond, Andrew, Harrison, Andre, Brandon, David, Leandro, Festus, James and Marreese.

Thank you for giving me something to cheer for. And thank you for giving me hope.

I emailed the letter to my brother, Chris, who had connections with the franchise and sent it directly to one of the team's executives. His response was immediate:

Thanks, Chris, for the email. I will pass it along TODAY to Coach Kerr, who I am sure will find a way to read it to the players (or put it on their chairs in the locker room). That is one of the best letters that I have ever read. I hope your sister makes it through this difficult time.

Mary and I began exchanging emails. She lived in Michigan and was only in the Bay Area when the Warriors had a long stretch of home games. She told me she knew about my letter to the team, and that her son told her the coach read it to them. "I admire your strength," she said. "Message me any time." Our messages were about basketball at first, and then gradually about deeper issues, such as faith and loss and strength. I had come to think of her as a friend, and she had come to address me as simply "Sis."

A good friend once asked me what helped me through the hardest times of my depression. Without hesitation, I answered, "Gardening and basketball." I was still on my journey, following Robby's path and learning new things. But gardening and basketball had been steady companions along the way. Gardening was easy to understand—it was peaceful and nurturing. It was enabling growth and life. Basketball was more of a surprise, though in the end it made sense to me. Love for a team is still, in the end, love. You cheer for them, you hope for the health and success of its team members, individually and collectively. You feel sadness when they are injured or have a bad night. You pull together with other people who share a passion for the team. And in the end, you are one of 20,000-plus screaming fans pouring their hearts out for their victory. It's a positive energy so electrifying that it ignites your senses and elevates your spirit. It reminds you that there is a force far more powerful than hate. And in this sense, I suppose it was similar to the power of prayer. Whatever god people pray to, or none at all, when you have groups of people pulling for you and sending you nothing but positivity, it carries you through. That is the power that humanity has when it is focused on one common goal. On love—and yes, basketball.

Chapter 29

Mothers and Sons

The room around us was scattered with toys, children's books and stuffed animals in an attempt to make children forget where they were: the district attorney's office. I thought of all the children who had come into this room, perhaps too young to understand that their mother, father or sibling had been killed. Too young to understand that the only reason they were here playing with these toys was because justice had yet to be served upon those who had changed their lives forever.

Amy Harris, our victim advocate, met us in the lobby when we arrived. "The room we were supposed to meet in is occupied, so we'll be going into another room today," she said. She led us into the space, pushing the toys to the side and clearing a path for us to take our seats. We would be meeting the prosecutor for the first time today, and Amy encouraged us to ask as many questions as we wanted. But I didn't have any that she could answer.

Could she tell me how this could happen to my son? How this could happen to our family? I wasn't interested in the details, the forensics, the evidence, the suspects. I wasn't interested in any of it because in the end, nothing changed the fact that Robby was gone. What good did it do me to know exactly how he died when the only thing that kept me going was remembering how he lived?

The door opened as a woman who looked to be in her early 50s walked in wearing a dark suit. She introduced herself to Cicero and me, apologizing that it had taken so long to schedule this meeting. "First of all, I want to say how sorry I am about your son," she said. "We're going to do everything we can to make sure the people responsible pay for what they did." She had a thick, white binder in front of her and I dreaded the thought of what those pages contained.

She gave us an overview of the case and what to expect next: a preliminary hearing, the trial, the sentencing phase. She explained that the preliminary hearing would be an abridged version of the whole trial, during which each side would present all the evidence. The judge would then determine if there was enough to proceed with a jury trial. We sat, listening to all of it, Cicero taking notes.

"Do you have any questions?" she asked.

"Do you think you have a strong case?" I asked. It was the only thing I could think of. I worried about the case getting dropped or the suspects going free because of lack of evidence. As if Robby's life and death were worthless.

"I do," she said. And that was enough for me.

The preliminary hearing had been scheduled, canceled and rescheduled twice already. More than six months came and went since that first meeting with the prosecutor. Amy had warned us this would happen. The defense would try to push the hearing back as far as possible. It was brutal. I would send group messages out to friends and family who were interested in attending the hearing. Then I would meditate, go for long walks, abuse the elliptical trainer at the gym, only to stuff my face that evening with chocolate and baked goods as a means of calming my nerves. By the eve of the scheduled hearing, we all walked around with our

nerves exposed like live wires, snapping at each other and retreat-
ing to our individual vices. And then, just like that, we would get
the word that the hearing was canceled. Again. We bounced from
one extreme to the other—from anxiety to relief, fear to comfort,
only to gear ourselves up for the next, unexpected wave of emotions set off by an email announcing a new hearing date.

That was the difference with this type of grief. There was an
added layer of complexity: the criminal justice system, the court
process, the investigation, the news—each one acting as an open
flame threatening to set whatever fibers of strength you've gathered on fire. Healing, re-traumatizing, accepting, hurting. It was
a merciless cycle that no human should ever have to endure. I was
stronger now, yes, by following Robby's lead and acquiring my own
coping tools along the way. But one unexpected issue continued to
linger, no matter how much I tried to ignore it: race.

⟿

I knew before we met with the prosecutor that the suspects were
described as three African American males. That was before I
learned of the additional Asian male who was Cora's nephew. I
didn't know the impact that had on me until one day when I was
walking from my car in a parking lot toward a building for my
therapy session. I looked behind me and saw three African American males walking together, laughing. A surge of panic went
through me, and before I knew it, I was running. Running as fast
as I could toward the building. It happened again when I went to a
grocery store and saw three other African American males walking
in the parking lot. I sat in my car and locked my doors until I was
sure they were gone.

I had never reacted this way before Robby's death. I didn't want
to be this person. The three men who killed my son had already

turned me into a grieving mother. I didn't want them to turn me into a racist grieving mother. And yet it had become instinctual. I was too ashamed to tell anyone about it, even during my therapy sessions. *I am not a racist. I am afraid of seeing three black males because three black males killed my son. And they are still out there.* That was what I told myself, and I hoped with all my being that it was true.

It was something that increasingly bothered me as race relations in the country were coming to a boiling point. There were more stories of the shooting deaths of unarmed black men by police in the news, and protests were cropping up in cities around the nation. I sympathized with all the victims and their mothers, and I shared in the growing frustration. And yet, I still wondered if I had seen those victims on the streets if I wouldn't run into a building as I had done when I saw those three men. I wondered if deep down I had taken the actions of these three men and used them to form a judgment against the whole race.

I continued to grapple with it internally, reasoning with myself, while also trying to understand from the outside looking in. If the suspects had been described as three white males, would I have had the same reaction seeing three white men together? I believed the answer was yes. If the suspects had been three Filipino men, how would I feel then? I imagined I would have felt more anger than fear. I would have seen more of my son in them. I would have felt as if I had known them more. And how could they do that to someone they looked like and had so much in common with? While I knew that was a generalization in itself, that was how I felt.

I continued to work on untangling my fear of the suspects from my fear of being a racist until it was clear to me after the arrests that my anxiety was rooted in the suspects themselves. I felt immediate relief knowing that when I saw three black males together, I wouldn't have to wonder if they were the three who killed my son.

I forced myself to think deeply and honestly about how I truly felt. With this type of tragedy, did it really matter what race a person was on either side? Did it make a perpetrator any more guilty if they were black, Asian, Latino or white? And did it make a victim's death any less tragic if they were of a certain race? No.

Unfortunately, everyday news told us otherwise.

⌒

Shortly after the arrests, I received an email regarding a problem with an account. The notice said I owed money, and that I had to call and schedule an appointment to dispute, discuss and/or make payment arrangements. This was the last thing I needed. I called the number on the letter, my irritation clearly coming through. "I want to make an appointment to dispute the balance," I said.

Cynthia West, the woman on the other end, let out a little snort. "You can't dispute it if we haven't even met yet."

I felt the heat rise to my head. "Then I want to meet with you so I can formally dispute it after our meeting," I said.

A few weeks later, I walked into her office, both of us standoffish. She went through my account and ticked off all the reasons her company had come to determine the amount of money I owed. I then stated all my reasons why I thought they were mistaken. She was all business, barely cracking a smile, looking at me as if she had seen and heard it all, and I was just another con artist. She clearly did not like me, and the feeling was mutual. It was a miracle that by the end of our verbal sparring, we had come to a compromise. She began processing my paperwork, and by then I had relaxed.

"Do you like the Warriors?" I asked, trying to fill the silence.

"I don't watch sports," she said, as she continued typing, not bothering to look up.

"Oh," I said.

Silence.

"I really like them," I said. "I wasn't really a sports fan either."

"Then why did you start watching them?" she asked.

I paused before answering. It was one of those questions I had to think a few steps ahead for, like when people asked me how many kids I had. Do I tell them the truth and make them uncomfortable, or do I lie to keep things casual? For some reason, I went for it.

"Because I lost my son and I was depressed. They were the only thing I could watch on TV, and sometimes the only thing that would get me out of bed."

The tapping of her keyboard stopped, and to my surprise, her eyes had welled up with tears. I told her about the letter I wrote to the team and how the coach read it to the players. I told her how I had become friends with one of the players' mothers and that we exchanged emails from time to time. I was crying now, too, as I told my story. Cynthia opened her top drawer and plopped a big box of tissues on her desk, both of us reaching to pull out a sheet.

"I am a cancer survivor," she said. She told me she was a single mother and she had to find strength for her son. "And I know what you mean about not being able to get out of bed. I had a girlfriend who would call and check on me every day. Sometimes you need that. Whatever it takes for you to get up and keep going. God does that for us." And then I felt our connection end.

"I don't know if I believe in God," I said. "I've pulled away from the church I was raised in, and I don't like hearing about God."

"I understand," she said. "But God loves you even if you don't realize it." She proceeded to quote a scripture, Psalms 61:2. It was her favorite, she said.

> *From the ends of the earth,*
> *I cry to you for help*

when my heart is overwhelmed.
Lead me to the towering rock of safety,
for you are my safe refuge.

I was moved. I wasn't instantly converted, but I was moved by her emotion and her belief. "You know, I didn't expect to like you," I told her.

She laughed. "You know, I woke up not wanting to come to this appointment!" We both laughed, tears still in our eyes. "Maybe you can come with me to my church sometime," she said. I was skeptical, but I liked her and I decided to give it a try.

I met Cynthia that following Sunday at a Christian church about 20 minutes from my home. It was unlike any church setting I had ever seen. Inside the large lobby, people were scuttling their children into one part of the facility where they would be separated in classrooms by age group. On the other end of the lobby was a coffee shop called "He Brew." I had to laugh.

"Pati!" Cynthia called out, walking over and hugging me. "Welcome!"

She introduced me to several people, all warm and welcoming. She took me by the arm and led me through the main entrance where she said they "worshipped." It was a large auditorium with a full stage, now occupied by a band playing their instruments. One large screen hung from center stage.

"Do you want to get coffee first?" she asked. I couldn't believe it. The Catholic Church would never encourage bringing coffee to Mass. In fact, I was told I wasn't supposed to eat before morning Mass.

"It's okay," I replied, still trying to find my bearings. This definitely wasn't the Buddhist monastery either. The band began to sing, the lyrics flashing on the huge screen above them. I felt stiff and awkward as people were raising their arms up, closing their eyes and singing along. I looked at Cynthia next to me, whose eyes were now closed and who was swaying back and forth. *What am I doing here?* I thought. This was a woman who was attempting to collect a debt—a debt I disputed—just a few days ago, and now I was with her at her church. The band sang a few more songs before a young man in jeans and a sweater came on stage.

"That's the pastor," Cynthia said.

"The pastor? In jeans?" I responded.

She laughed.

I watched and listened to him as he walked from one end of the stage to the other, connecting with the audience. He was casual as he spoke, as if he was addressing a group of old friends. He shared a story of how he had forced himself to go to medical school with the hope of one day having a lucrative career—money being his main objective. It was only after one failing grade after another that he realized he wasn't cut out for the profession. He realized he was veering from whatever it was he was meant to do in life because he was focused only on money. "So what is it that *you* are on this Earth to do? And have you veered away from that?" he asked.

Dramatic pause.

"What is *your* true purpose?"

Cynthia nodded and yelled out "Yes!" throughout his sermon, tears running down her cheeks. She was feeling it—and at some point, so was I. I took notes, wanting to remember his statements. Before I knew it, it was over.

"That's it?" I asked Cynthia.

"I told you, this isn't Catholic church!"

There wasn't a heavy emphasis on Jesus or God or destiny, though I believe that was a given for everyone else there. The message was about accountability and choices. It placed the action in our hands, and I liked that.

I met with her again at her church. She came to my home a few times, and I took her with me hiking. When she didn't hear from me, she'd send me a text message asking if I was okay. She knew a trial was coming, and she said she would pray for me and my family.

As my friendship with Cynthia grew, I received a message from my old college friend Audrea, whom I hadn't heard from in nearly two decades.

"Call me! We have so much to catch up on!"

I called her the next morning, both of us picking up where we had left off, as if no time had passed. She had five children now, ranging in age from twentysomething to three years old. She actually did start her own magazine, called MotherWit, based in Sacramento, while also working full time as a director at an organization focused on higher education. I told her about Robby, whom she only remembered as a young boy. "Oh, Pati," she said. "Your baby. I'm so sorry." She asked me to write a commentary on my experience as a grieving mother so she could publish it in her magazine, which I did.

We continued to message each other, reigniting our old friendship, planning to meet somewhere in the middle someday so we could see each other again. I shared stories about her with Cicero as we were driving somewhere, explaining that she had been one of my best friends my last year in college.

"Isn't it strange?" I said. "Three young black men, three sons, took Robby's life away. And now three black women, three mothers, have come into my life, nurturing me, healing me, giving me comfort."

I was referring to Mary, the Warriors mom; Cynthia, the single mom; and now Audrea, the mother of five. It was an overly simplistic statement, I knew, but it meant something to me. It was the balance in the universe that I had messaged Cora about. Three sons who had taken so much from us, whose lives at some point had taken a turn. Three mothers all trying to raise their sons with strength and integrity, now helping me along my journey. It wasn't about race, I knew. There was good and bad, no matter what ethnicity, gender, sexual preference or demographic slice people fell into. What these women showed me was that for every act of hate, there is an act of love. And oftentimes, that was far more powerful.

"Love isn't love until you give it away," Mary often said. And I was grateful for the gift.

Purpose

Chapter 30

Mothers and Movements

It seemed no matter where I turned, I couldn't escape the issue of gun violence. This became even more true once the election season started. Tears were streaming down my face as I sat in front of the television. Nine women stood shoulder to shoulder on the blue-carpeted stage, facing the passionate crowd at the 2016 Democratic National Convention—and the millions of Americans like me who had a deep, personal stake in the outcome of the election. It had been a particularly ugly presidential campaign, with Republican presidential nominee Donald Trump extolling the virtues of the Second Amendment and Democratic nominee Hillary Clinton expressing the dire need for common-sense gun laws.

I went over the arguments repeatedly in my head, but I could never understand why the former was seen as a sacrifice for the latter. Why was it that any effort to keep guns out of the hands of dangerous people, potentially saving innocent lives, was seen as an affront to responsible gun owners and their right to bear arms? People's opinions, including those of my friends and family, fell along party lines, red and blue—all or nothing. But it deserved more than that. It was an issue that transcended political parties. People were dying. Every day, 306 people in America are shot in murders, assaults, suicides and suicide attempts, unintentional shootings, and police intervention. Every day, 90 people die from gun violence. When a loved one becomes just another number in those statistics, they start to mean something. But it shouldn't have to come to that.

We knew that the weapons used in Robby's killing were bought illegally off the streets, and that after the incident one of the suspects sold his gun, putting it right back on the streets. It was an endless, deadly cycle that neither presidential candidate had a personal connection to, in order to truly understand. But these women on the stage did. They called themselves the Mothers of the Movement—women whose children had died from gun violence. They were African American women, and most of their children had died at the hands of police and gang members. I recognized each victim's name: Oscar Grant, Eric Garner, Jordan Davis, Michael Brown, Sandra Bland, Trayvon Martin, Dontre Hamilton, Hadiya Pendleton and Blair Holt. Their children's tragic deaths had ignited a heated national debate about police reform and race relations, and gave rise to the Black Lives Matter movement. I understood and appreciated the added layers of complexity to their cause—race and a system that, more and more, seemed stacked against them.

"You don't stop being a parent when your child dies," said Lucia McBath, whose 17-year-old son, Jordan Davis, was shot and killed in Jacksonville, Florida, in 2012. "I am still Jordan Davis' mother. His life ended the day he was shot and killed for playing loud music. But my job as his mother didn't." I nodded my head as she spoke, feeling grateful that she was able to put into words the same pain I had been feeling.

Another mother, Christine Leinonen, took the stage during the convention. She was the mother of Christopher "Drew" Leinonen, one of the 49 victims of the June 12, 2016, mass shooting at Pulse, a gay nightclub in Orlando, Florida. She shared the story of how she, as a state trooper, had to turn in her service weapon when she went into labor with her son. "The weapon that murdered my son fires 30 rounds in one minute. An Orlando city commissioner pointed out the terrible math. One minute per gun to fire so many shots, five minutes per bell to honor so many lives. I'm glad common-sense gun policy was in place when Christopher was born, but where was that common sense the day he died?" she asked.

My son's death was not the same as their sons' deaths. He was not an unarmed black man. He was not pulled over or racially profiled. He was not killed in a mass shooting. He was not the victim of anyone attempting to make a political or social statement. His death was not a high-profile news story that captured national headlines. But he was my son and I was his mother, and his life ended because someone who should not have had a gun did. And that common thread, that common loss, made their cause my own.

Shooting deaths are on the news practically every night. They play like gun scenes we have become so accustomed, addicted and drawn to in action movies. I worked at four different daily newspapers during my journalism career and at each one the mantra was the same: *If it bleeds, it leads.* That's what commanded the placement of our stories. But for those of us who have lost a loved one to gun violence, each story serves as a merciless reminder, a reopening and deepening of wounds. You think of the victim. You imagine the call that will be made to the victim's next of kin. You remember the call you got. You think of the shock that will ensue and the long, lingering pain that will ebb and flow like the phantom pain of a lost limb. You think of the tremendous waste of life. You think of your own child. And at each point, you just want the stories to stop.

These women's speeches both pained and inspired me because, despite their personal tragedies, they were there on my TV screen, taking a stand on the largest, most prominent platform in the country at that very moment. They were fighting so that no parent or child would suffer the same tragedies they did.

I thought about the pastor at Cynthia's church, and the questions he posed: *What is* your *true purpose? What is it that* you *are on this Earth to do?*

⌁

California Lieutenant Governor Gavin Newsom had been campaigning aggressively for Proposition 63, the 2016 Background Checks for Ammunition Purchases and Large-Capacity Ammunition Magazine Ban. It was a crucial proposition aimed at closing loopholes in existing gun legislation. I agreed with it in its entirety, but one part in particular interested me. In 2014, voters passed Proposition 47, which made stealing an item that is valued at less than $950 a misdemeanor. Therefore, stealing a gun valued at less than $950 is a misdemeanor. Proposition 63 would make stealing a gun, including one valued at less than $950, a felony punishable by up to three years in prison.

The prosecutor handling Robby's case informed us the weapon that killed him had never been found, but that many guns in homicides were either sold illegally or stolen. For me, this was the crux of the problem in many cities, the problem of illegal guns on the streets. I wasn't against the Second Amendment. Robby owned some guns of his own, each of which he bought and registered legally. He loved to go target shooting with his friends and his dad. This was not that. This was focusing on the problems, the source of gun violence in the streets.

I slowly became more active in the cause, making donations, signing up for updates from the Brady Campaign to Prevent Gun Violence and forwarding information to friends and family on social media. And when Senator Christopher S. Murphy of Connecticut filibustered for 15 hours on the Senate floor on gun control, ending at 2:30 a.m. on June 16, 2016, I felt compelled to reach out.

I went to the senator's website, sharing my story and expressing gratitude for his leadership and commitment. Mine was the first comment following the filibuster, after which another person posted: "My mom was stabbed. Should we ban knives?" Another common argument was that more people just needed to be armed. Good guys versus bad guys, just like the Wild West. And yet, so many police officers had lost their lives in recent news. Were they not the most armed and the most trained of us all?

I looked for the local chapters of Parents of Murdered Children and The Compassionate Friends and marked their monthly meetings in my phone calendar. I reached out to the campaign strategists for Prop. 63 and offered myself as a voice, either in writing or through interviews. But I didn't feel it was enough.

I met with Mario Chesney, an old friend of mine whom I had known since middle school. After graduating from high school, he went straight into the Marines, then went through the police academy and served in law enforcement in a nearby city that faced its own regular headlines on local homicides. At one point he worked undercover in the gang unit, growing his hair and sporting tattoos in an effort to look more like a gangster. He had been retired now for a couple of years after suffering an injury.

"I don't know what my plan is, but I want to help make Vallejo better," I said to him over the phone. We met for breakfast as I rattled off ideas. A foundation for Robby. Helping youth. Providing more opportunities. Addressing gun violence. No matter what idea I came up with, it always came back to that.

"Vallejo doesn't have a gun buyback program," he said. "That would be effective in getting some of these guns out of circulation.

You'll get a lot of old guns and guns that aren't even working, but even if you can just get one illegal gun that can cause damage, think of how many lives that may save."

I went home and did research, discovering a news article from 2013, the one year there was a gun buyback event in Vallejo. It was made possible by a one-time grant. "What happens after the police department gets the guns?" I asked Mario.

"They get melted down in a warehouse," he replied.

Three years before Robby was killed I spent a weekend immersed in Vallejo's downtown area where there was a growing artists' community. The area had long been plagued by drugs, prostitution and violence, and the hope was that the artists would begin to revive the area. The article was never published, but it allowed me to see the potential changes the artists brought.

"What if the melted guns are given to the artists in Vallejo and they can transform them into art?" I asked, thinking out loud.

I was already thinking ahead. Every year we could have an art exhibit called "The Art of Peace," featuring art made with melted-down guns. Guns that could have potentially killed people, now transformed into something beautiful for everyone to enjoy. I would partner with the police department, leaders of the art community and city officials. I would form a foundation and secure grants for two annual events: the gun buyback program and the art exhibit. And then I thought of Robby's welding and the weld shop that was dedicated to him at his work. Part of the materials from the melted guns could be used for vocational training, giving people skills that would make them more employable. The guns would be transformed into weapons of hope and opportunity. There would be a lot of work to do, a lot of people to meet with. A lot of planning and executing that I would have to squeeze in between my regular job and the upcoming trial. It would require that I put aside my fear and finally return to the city I had avoided for two years. But now I had a reason to return. Good or bad, I didn't want to focus on my trauma anymore. I didn't want to keep revisiting what caused me pain. Because now I had a purpose.

Diagnoses
  ACUTE POSTTRAUMATIC STRESS DISORDER – Primary
  Telephone Encounter: Called patient to check on progress with the sertraline, but it looks like patient hasn't picked up prescription. UNABLE TO REACH PATIENT BY PHONE.

Chapter 31

Forgiveness

My cellphone buzzed forcing it to inch sideways. I was on a conference call. I slowly pushed my seat away from my desk and reached over to the table behind me to pick it up, careful not to disconnect my headset from my computer. With my back twisted, my left arm and right leg extended and my right hand keeping my headset firmly on my head, I was now in some sort of strange, seated yoga pose. I tilted the top of my phone upward and squinted at the screen until the message came into focus: *The judge has confirmed the preliminary hearing date. It is scheduled for 9:00 am in Dept 15 in Vallejo. I'm assuming it will last probably two days, potentially more.*

I stared at the screen as my boss's voice continued traveling from the headset to my ears. But all I could hear was the warbled sound of the teacher in those "Peanuts" cartoons. *Here we go again*, I thought. Only this time, it would not be postponed.

Ruben, Cicero and I met with the lead prosecutor in the case weeks before the scheduled hearing. There had been staffing changes in the DA's office since the first meeting we had, and this was the first time we were meeting with the new prosecutor handling Robby's case. He was tall and well-dressed, intense and thorough in his explanations of the process and the evidence. I had a lot of questions this time: *What are the biggest challenges to the case? If the judge decides there's enough evidence to go to trial, will they try to get plea bargains? When would the jury trial begin? Have any witnesses come forward? What will their defense be?*

And finally: *Do we really have to be at the preliminary hearing?*

It was at that point that Ruben looked up. He had been slumped on the chair to my left, head down, his right hand over his left in an attempt to calm his nerves. Cicero was sitting in a chair to my right, listening and taking notes. He had taken on the role knowing that Ruben and I were too emotional to keep track of everything. This was hard for all of us, but I worried most about Ruben. Up until now he hadn't met with anyone at the DA's office, opting instead to let me take the lead. He didn't want to know, and neither did I.

"That's up to you," said the prosecutor.

After our meeting, he walked us over to the courthouse across the street so he could show us the courtroom for the preliminary hearing and the trial. We went through the metal detectors and down a long hallway.

"Here it is," he said, turning the doorknob of a dark brown door. Inside were rows of blue fabric chairs facing the front of the court where the judge would sit and witnesses would take the stand. "This is where the defendants will all be sitting," he said, walking to a table not far from the blue chairs. "This is where your family should sit." We looked at the seats, with no separation in the middle.

"Where will their families go?" I asked. He pointed to the chairs at the end of the row, which meant they would need to pass us to get in and out of their seats. I looked at the table where the defendants would be, merely a few footsteps away.

"Again, it's up to you if you want to come to the hearing. I would want you there for the jury trial on some days, but the hearing is up to you," he reiterated.

One year had passed since the arrests were made. Two years since Robby's death. In that time, I went back and forth over whether I would attend the hearing and the trial. I shared my anxieties with Julie, asking her opinion and how she felt about going. "Nothing that happens in that courtroom can hurt us any more than they already have," she responded. It was a response that filled me with pride and pain.

I thought of whether I would address the defendants if given the chance, and what I would say. I would take long drives, going over what message I would possibly want to leave them with as they prepared to carry out their sentences. Some days, my message would be one of compassion and forgiveness. It would start with something like: *Seeing your suffering does not ease my own suffering. It has never been my goal or our family's goal to seek revenge. Instead, I will focus on forgiveness, even if you do not seek it. Forgiveness so that we can ease our pain and be free to honor Robby. Forgiveness so that we can live our lives through love and not hate.*

Other days, the message was focused more on letting them know who Robby was, the life he was living and what they took away when they decided in that instant that that day would be his last. *Robby did not deserve to die. He deserved to live his life, pursue his many dreams, make mistakes and learn from them. He deserved to grow old, looking back and appreciating the full arc of his life. You took that from him, and you took that from us. You will never realize how deeply and how broadly you changed all our lives that day.*

I thought a lot about the notion of closure. Since the arrests were made, I was told repeatedly that this would be the beginning of closure. But it wasn't. It wasn't closure for us; it was closure for *them* and their families. This was when their fates would be decided. Robby's fate was decided for him the day he was killed. They were facing first-degree-murder charges, among a list of other charges. The DA's office was pushing for sentences of 50 years to life. I thought about the jury reading a guilty verdict—*if* they reached a guilty verdict. And when I thought of that, what I wanted to say to them was this:

I know that many people may think that today marks one of closure for me and our family. I am grateful for all the great work of the investigators, the DA's office, the jury and the judge in ensuring that justice was served. But this does not bring me closure. Closure for me would have been watching my son continue to grow into a man. Watching him find his passion, working hard and building a life for himself. Watching him meet the person he would marry. Crying at his wedding and telling him how much I loved him and how very proud I was of him. Watching him become a father and playing with my grand-children. Watching him buy his boat and traveling the world, by sea and by plane, as he had always wanted. Then, spending my days with my crepe-like skin and silver hair, content to leave this earth knowing that he and his sister had families of their own, and that they would be okay. Closure for me would have been saying goodbye to him as I faded gently away, telling him how very honored I had been to be his mother.

I will never get that closure.

Only I have the power to give myself closure now, and that will be through forgiveness. I do not believe that any of you were born with hate in your heart. You were born as Robby was, with inno-cence and openness. I cannot judge you for the decisions you've made, but I can try to forgive you knowing that you are human and are worthy of compassion.

Chapter 32

Going Before the Judge

My heart raced as I walked through security at the building. I walked through the metal detector and waited at the other end as the security guard went through the contents of my purse. Julie and I were running late that morning and ran even later as we struggled to find parking in the rain.

"Here you go," said the guard, handing me my purse. I ran toward the steps, seeing Cicero and our family members waiting. My mom was standing, wringing her hands with worry.

"I thought you weren't going to make it," Cicero said. The building was busy that day, people walking from one office to the other, one meeting place to another.

"We have to go," said Cicero. I took his hand, both of our palms sweaty. We listened as someone explained the process to us, where we should go and where the judge would be. A photographer showed up and followed us to meet the judge, a woman named Jane with a shock of white hair. The photographer whispered something in her ear, and the judge nodded her head. We ran to gather our family members, herding them to the area where we were told to stand and wait for the judge. My heartbeat was bouncing off the marble floors and polished walls of the cavernous building.

I looked at Cicero as the judge made her way in our direction, her black robe flowing behind her as she walked. "I'd like to start by asking you to join me in a moment of silence for Robby," she said. I bowed my head, shutting my lids tightly to keep the tears from coming. I knew it was an unorthodox move for the judge. She lifted her head after about one minute and slowly began to speak.

> *We are gathered here in the presence of these witnesses for the purpose of uniting in matrimony Cicero and Pati. The contract of marriage is most solemn and is not to be undertaken lightly, but thoughtfully and seriously, with a realization of its obligations and responsibilities. Cicero, Pati, this civil ceremony is meant to confirm what the two of you have already decided to do, and that is to marry each other. No words of mine or any other person truly marry you. You actually marry each other when you exchange your vows and you commit yourselves to this union ...*

We stood there under San Francisco City Hall's grand dome with our family members forming a circle around us. It was not the wedding we had planned for two years ago, but we were not the same people. The world and our lives had changed. I thought about the building we were in, where San Francisco Mayor George Moscone and Supervisor Harvey Milk were assassinated in 1978. The tragedy had become a part of the building's story, though many who entered it were too young to remember. For the unknowing, all they saw was the beauty in the architecture, the strength in the marble, the integrity in its purpose. For many, the building was not famous for the assassinations, but for the hundreds of same-sex marriages that took place in it, ushering in a new era of civil liberties for couples around the nation, and sparking the slogan "Love Is Love."

For us, it was both—a somber structure that housed tragedy, pain and loss—and a refurbished work of art that reflected resilience, strength and love. I felt all of it that day, and the significance of our wedding site was not lost on me. I appreciated how far I had come, and I accepted that I now lived with a lifelong heartache, sometimes dull and lingering, other times merciless and unrelenting in its attacks. I, too, housed both pain and resilience, loss and love. But in the past two years, I learned that we are stronger than we know.

What saved me initially was my will to live on for my daughter, but I realized that that placed an enormous burden on her. You cannot rest your whole reason for being on the shoulders of another person. It denies you both your freedom. Your potential. Your life, as it should be lived. I had to want to live for myself. And that desire returned when I realized that we are more supported and loved than we realize. That in the face of hate, the only answer is to love.

In the darkness of my despair, I was unable to see the acts of kindness that lifted me up. I could only hear the offensive words. The offensive silence. But there were also gestures—large and small. A package of tea from a friend who said, "I heard tea helps soothe the soul. I hope it helps soothe yours." A phone call from a long-lost friend who said merely, "I don't know what to say, but I would like to cook for you." Two small paintings of my dogs made by the hands of a friend clear across the country. And prayers. Even if I had lost my faith, I knew that friends and family were praying for us and for Robby. And that somehow those prayers gave us strength.

I have followed my son's path, seeking a way to heal and ways to understand and forgive. I have studied different religions through his books, entered different churches and explored spirituality beyond dogma, finally realizing that at the core of every practice, the same basic tenets emerge for those willing to see them: kindness, forgiveness and compassion. This is what Robby came to understand, and what I understood now.

I pushed myself to do things I would have never done before, especially if I felt fear, with the hope that I would find life again—within and around me. I felt and continue to feel profound sadness and a deep loss. But I also feel gratitude, happiness and even hope. Hope that enabled me to exchange vows of marriage and envision a future with Cicero—even in the midst of a looming trial. And I have learned that it is all okay.

People told me not to cry because Robby is in a better place. There is no way for me to know if that is true, though more often than not, I have faith that it is. And I have faith that I will see him again. What I do know is that while I am still alive, I have a purpose. I can play a part in making it a better place *here*—for myself, for my family, for people I may never meet. And for Robby.

There is a quote etched into his bronze and granite marker at the cemetery that was taken from a message he wrote to his girl-friend at the time. After his funeral she sent it to me, saying only that "he had the biggest heart." It is a message that has sustained me the past two years—and one that will continue to remind me that even in his brief time, he continues to lead the way.

> *Love is following your heart, not your fears. God will show you the way and will heal your wounds. I think that is my purpose in this world. I know that's why I'm here, to help those who need it even if they don't know it. One day you will be freed from all the things that imprison you, even fear.*
>
> *Because love conquers all.*

Looking Forward

A row of cream-colored officers' mansions along Walnut Avenue on Mare Island stands as stately as ever. Though they have not been occupied by naval officers and their families in decades, the homes possess an elegance of a bygone era with their massive, plantation-style porches and proud pillars. Today, like many structures on the former naval shipyard, the mansions are enjoying a renaissance of sorts. A few of them have been converted to office spaces offering different services. Elsewhere on Mare Island new businesses have come in, including a film studio, a local brewery, a company that manufactures "tiny houses" and a former coal shed that now houses a colorful mix of studio spaces. Here, local artists have breathed new life into the industrial space, setting up their wall art, mixed media, pottery and other forms of artistic expression.

On June 30, 2017, a crowd of more than 320 people—from local politicians to law enforcement agencies to artists to members of local unions and community organizations—gathered behind Vino Godfather, a wine-tasting room that occupies one of the officers' mansions along with its massive courtyard behind the structure. At 6:00 p.m., the sun was still high, and guests arrived dressed in summer social attire, save for those in law enforcement who came in full uniform. My mouth was dry, and my face felt tight from sunburn.

Nearly two and a half years had gone by without me setting foot in Vallejo, and now here I was on Mare Island—the closure of which I had blamed for everything that had gone wrong in the city. This was the place I had chosen for the official launch of The Robby Poblete Foundation. For weeks I worried that no one would come. Why would they? I had practically been in hiding since Robby's death and now I was asking them for support. "If we're lucky," I told members of the foundation's board of directors, "we'll get about 100 people."

"This looks like more than 100 people," said Mike Jory, my scarecrow and now a member of our board of directors. My nerves were raw, but for the first time it was a positive thing. I scanned the crowd—Cora and her husband, who had flown in from Hawaii. Our friendship had endured, allowing her to support me, and allowing me to be grateful for that support. Julie had her hands full helping our team of volunteers, registering people as they lined up to get their programs and auction paddles. Ruben was sitting underneath the shade of a large tree, taking in the enormity of the event. "I think you've hit a homerun," he said, walking over to me. "Look at all these people." Robby's co-workers from Genentech had their own table, some of them dabbing their eyes as they looked at the huge flag that met guests at the entrance that read: *The Robby Poblete Foundation. Be the Change.* Cicero, now also a board member, kept busy greeting people and making sure I was okay and later surprised me by giving his own speech to the crowd.

Those who couldn't make it were sure to send messages and donations, including Neric and Phill, from the Philippines, and Katsu, from Japan. "I'm so sorry to miss this, but I'm so proud of what you have done," wrote Cynthia. I smiled reading the message, remembering that first, tense meeting with her as she attempted to collect a debt. The Golden State Warriors won the NBA Finals two weeks prior to the event, so Mary returned to her hometown

in Michigan and was unable to attend, but sent her usual words
of support that I had come to rely on for inspiration. And Audrea,
my college friend whom I had recently reconnected with, made the
hour-plus drive from Sacramento just to come and give me a hug.
All the new friends I had made along the way were there, joined by
friends whom I thought I had lost in my grief.

This was our official foundation launch and the first of what
would become an annual fundraiser. Our emcees announced the
first in a line of speakers for our launch event. Vallejo Mayor Bob
Sampayan took the stage holding a file and his speech. He called
me to come stand beside him and began to read a Proclamation
Against Gun Violence, which he wrote specifically for this event. I
took the stage and looked out at the massive crowd before us as he
began to read:

> *Whereas, gun violence has affected the lives of Valle-*
> *joans and residents of our nation with senseless and*
> *needless injuries and deaths; and*
>
> *Whereas, 40 percent of victims of gun violence in*
> *Vallejo are between the ages of 26 and 40 years; and*
>
> *Whereas, today, we honor the memories of the*
> *victims and the grief of their survivors; and*
>
> *Whereas, we, as a community, believe there are*
> *ways to take unwanted firearms off the streets so that*
> *they will not be used as hostile tools of violence; and*
>
> *Whereas, through The Robby Poblete Foundation,*
> *these unwanted firearms can become symbols of hope*
> *in an annual community gun buyback program; and*
>
> *Whereas, the firearms will then be melted and*
> *sculpted into artwork by local artists and will be*
> *placed in a local exhibit entitled "Art of Peace"; and*
>
> *Whereas, funds will also be used to provide*

vocational skills for those in need of job training in welding and metal fabrication, which was Robby's vocation; and

Now, therefore, be it proclaimed that I, Bob Sampayan, mayor of the City of Vallejo, and the Vallejo City Council, do hereby support the work of The Robby Poblete Foundation and its effort to stem the tide of gun violence and proclaim today, June 30, 2017, as Robby Poblete Day in his honor.

The mayor handed me the proclamation, tears in his eyes. We embraced as each guest rose from their chair and gave a lengthy applause. And I realized, this community was my home.

It was always my home.

⌐

After writing the last page of this book, I felt the urge to turn my idea into something tangible. And so I started with a mission—the backbone upon which I was able to build out the rest of the foundation's structural bones. I filed all the legal paperwork, selected members for our board of directors and put together a three-year strategy. And then the flesh—the foundation's programs. How I would carry them out. Who the stakeholders and partners would be. Foundations and potential donors we would need to approach. Then, finally, the soul: Robby. At the core of each program, from the micro to the macro level, Robby's story was woven into the DNA.

The mission was simple: to get unwanted firearms out of circulation through an annual gun buyback program and transform them into instruments of hope and opportunity through art and vocational skills programs. The gun buyback was obvious. Robby was killed by a person who obtained a firearm illegally—approximately 70,000 firearms a year are stolen from homes in California alone. Gun buybacks would allow people to dispose of their unwanted guns in a safe and efficient manner, thus eliminating the chances of them falling into the wrong hands. After the buyback, the local police would screen the weapons for their serial numbers, then send them off to a company where they will be dismantled and turned into scrap metal.

But, for me, it didn't end there. I didn't want the story of our foundation to be about destruction. I wanted it to be about transformation—and life.

The Art of Peace program involves taking the scrap metal from the collected firearms and giving them to local artists to transform the materials into art. We issued a call for entries and received numerous proposals—from an artist in Russia, to another in Florida who was deeply affected by the mass shooting at Pulse nightclub, to a Bay Area artist who along with friends fled the political turmoil and violence in Iran, only to have those friends shot and killed in Brooklyn.

Lastly, I wanted to take Robby's love of welding and create a vocational skills program for those unwilling or unable to go to college. While the foundation bears Robby's name, I had to think deeply about those who perpetrated the crime. What opportunities could have prevented them from choosing this life? And so I began meeting with program directors in jails and at juvenile hall. I began tapping former connections from my time as a journalist, exploring ways to build awareness about opportunities in skilled trades and helping through the process of apprenticeship, certification and job placement foster youth who are about to age out. I met regularly with leaders of local labor unions and county recruiters for youth employment. Then one day I found myself going to Vallejo—first to meet with a group of community leaders whom

I had invited to participate in a stakeholders meeting as a means of introducing my ideas for The Robby Poblete Foundation. Then again, to meet with community leaders one-on-one. Afterward, I began going regularly, driving through streets that were filled with memories of my own childhood. Of my children's childhoods.

Shortly after launching the foundation, a local reporter asked me what it felt like to return to Vallejo. What kept me away, and what brought me back. I told him, "I couldn't bear driving down the same freeway toward a city that only reminded me of tragedy. But now I am driving toward hope."

In just 11 months, the foundation achieved everything I had set out to accomplish in three years, and it continues to gain momentum. To date, The Robby Poblete Foundation has:

- Held two gun buybacks in two counties, Solano and Contra Costa, getting 250 firearms out of circulation, several of which were assault weapons;

- Launched our Art of Peace, which will take the materials from the collected firearms and transform them into pieces of art to raise awareness about gun violence. Our call for entries attracted submissions from around the world, inspired the launch of an Art of Peace program headed by the Alameda County DA's office, and garnered much media attention, including three special news segments on local TV station KTVU Fox 2 News;

- Partnered with local labor union leaders, our county Office of Education, Workforce Development Board, and County Superior Court's Parole and Reentry Office to launch our Work in Progress program, which seeks to address an underlying cause of crime: lack of opportunity. We continue to raise awareness about the many opportunities in skilled trades, including paid apprenticeships, and sponsor apprentices who cannot afford the costs of work boots, books, transportation and other associated costs of an apprenticeship. We've sponsored two career fairs focused on apprenticeships in the trades and are helping at-risk youth, young adults and ex- offenders get into paid apprenticeship programs.

The foundation has been a welcome outlet for me, as the jury trial still has not taken place. The court dates have been delayed at least three times since the suspects were arrested. The trial is now set for May 2018, nearly four years since Robby's shooting. And while people have commended me for starting the foundation, I know that it has helped save me. I don't know what lies ahead, nor do I spend much time poring over the details of the case in preparation for the trial. I have accepted that what was done to my son and what will happen to those who took his life are completely out of my hands. So instead, I have chosen to focus on things that I can change for the better—as much as I can, for as long as I can.

In the face of tragedy, I have chosen to find peace.

~

To learn more about The Robby Poblete Foundation, go to www.robbypobletefoundation.org.

Acknowledgments

It was impossible to write this story without leaving out the names of many people who were a part of this journey—loved ones, new friends, old friends and people I only came into contact with once. Because of my initial shock and subsequent PTSD and anxiety, my eyes and my heart weren't fully open to all the support and love that people were offering me—both up close and from afar. I know now that it was this network of people that provided a spiritual safety net for me. That carried me through even when I felt completely alone. This was obviously not just my story. Everyone in my family and those among Robby's closest friends each had their own story to tell, their own feelings of loss, anger, grief and resilience. But theirs were not my stories to tell. For this reason, I chose to write from my experience alone without attempting to speak for anyone else. Because everyone's grief is unique.

To my daughter, Julie, thank you for being my light. You had to grow up so much faster than you should have, but you've done so with enormous grace and strength. I know your brother is so proud of you. This book is for you, as much as it is for him.

To my husband, Cicero. Nothing is as it was supposed to be, and yet you never wavered. I am grateful that you were a part of

Robby's life, and that you are forever a part of mine. Despite everything, it is a beautiful life with you in it.

To Ruben, thank you for allowing me to share our son's story. I see him every time I look at you, and I am grateful for that. You are and always will be family.

To my family members—Mom, Chris, Sandy, Jamelyn, Robert, Justin, Auntie Bing, Andrew, Kevin, Dave, Caroline, Mama Loli, Papa, Jim, Chelle, Lor, Lou, Frankie, Jeanette, the Estrella, Pabonan, Santos and Dionisio families—who rushed to my side and were there for all the prayers and gatherings. I know it wasn't always easy. You didn't know what to say or do, but I know you were always there waiting for me to say the word. To my friends—Leila Devine, Connie Gamoras, Annamarie Guila, Valerie Perez, Margie DeLeon, Girlie Panganiban, Mario Chesney, Alan Caragan and Cora Mendoza—thank you for the messages, the phone calls, the gifts, the simple reminders that you're thinking about me. To Rich Gamoras, who remained confident that I would turn my grief into something positive. To my new lifelong friend, Josette Lacey. To Robby's friends, Chez, William, Mark, Farrah, Vincent, thank you, thank you for bringing him joy. To my early readers, Jennifer Mitchell, Melissa Fondakowski, Eva Konigsberg and especially Levi Sumagaysay, who doubled as a supportive friend and my personal editor, thank you so much for all the solicited advice.

To Katsu Iha, *arigatou gozaimasu,* my dear friend. To Phillip Fullon, *salamat* for always finding a way to make me smile. And to Neric Acosta for showing me what a bike ride in heaven must feel like.

To Nothing But the Truth Publishing, especially Christine Bronstein and Mickey Nelson, for seeing the need for a book like this in the world and the need for diverse voices in the industry.

To the mothers I have met who have also lost their sons or daughters to violent crime, who are also navigating their own paths of pain and perseverance. We call ourselves the "Angel Moms." We are members of a club that no one wants to be in, and yet we remain resilient in honor of our children. May we continue to tell our stories.

And to Robby. I felt like you wrote this story with me. There were times when I thought I knew what I was going to write, and then something completely different emerged. I believe this was you, guiding my heart, my mind and my fingers to write the story you wanted to share. Thank you for continuing to teach me how to live.

31901062967403

CPSIA information can be obtained
at www.ICGtesting.com
Printed in the USA
LVOW03s0419190418
574027LV00001B/1/P